Accidental
AUTHOR

*If an ex-footballer, non-reader, personal trainer
and non-academic with no experience or qualifications
can write best-selling books then you can too!
You will be ready to write your own best-seller
before you finish reading this book.*

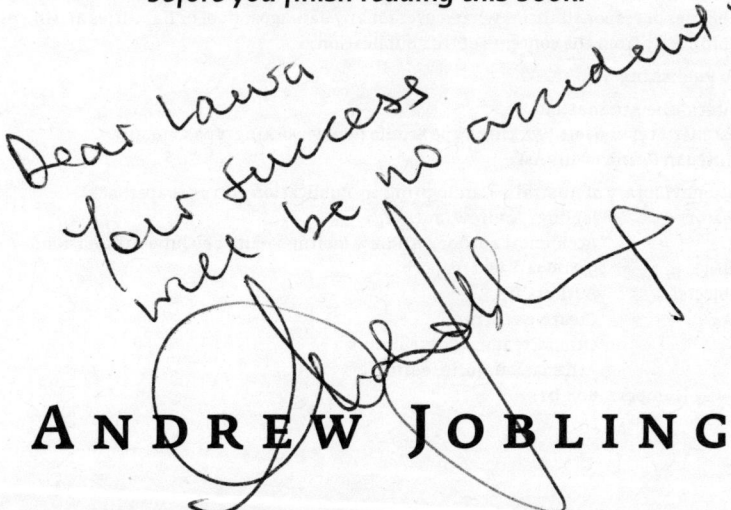

Dear Laura
Your success
will be no accident!

A N D R E W   J O B L I N G

JoJo
PUBLISHING

Accidental Author
Andrew Jobling

Published by Classic Author and Publishing Services Pty Ltd.
Imprint of JoJo Publishing.
First published 2015

'Yarra's Edge'
2203/80 Lorimer Street
Docklands VIC 3008
Australia

Email: admin@classic-jojo.com or visit www.classic-jojo.com

JoJo Publishing

Editor: Julie Athanasiou
Designer / typesetter: Working Type Studio (www.workingtype.com.au)
Printed in China by InkAsia

National Library of Australia Cataloguing-in-Publication entry : (paperback)
Creator: Jobling, Andrew, author.
Title: Accidental author / Andrew Jobling ; edited by Julie Athanasiou.
ISBN: 9780994183811 (paperback)
Subjects: Authorship.
                  Creative writing.
                  Other Creators/Contributors:
                  Athanasiou, Julie, editor.
Dewey Number: 808.02

Contents

Introduction

"I truly believe there are no accidents in life. We attract everything that we get — seemingly accidental or not!"

Many people, who achieve any sort of success, do it accidentally!

In 1905 an eleven-year-old became an accidental inventor when, on a freezing cold winter's night, he left a mixture of soda powder and water on his porch with a stirring stick in it. When Frank Epperson woke the next day he found it had become an ice lollipop. Several years later he patented this ice lollipop and founded the Popsicle Corporation.

In 1981 a nine-year-old boy accidentally ran through a plate glass door and completely severed the calf muscle in his left leg. He was rushed to the hospital and doctors stitched him back together. Luckily there was no permanent damage. He was not a swimmer, but kicking in the water was the only thing he could do to rehabilitate and get strength back into his leg. Three rehab sessions per week in the pool turned into three swimming squad sessions per week. Kieren Perkins went on to become the best 1500m swimmer in Australia and one of the all time greatest in the world and all because he accidentally ran through a plate glass door!

Why do so many accidents lead to success? Because, when we are in deliberate pursuit of a goal or dream we often quit before we get anywhere near its successful fulfillment — being human we have a tendency to be overly self-critical and self-doubting about our ability to achieve 'success'.

We analyse, we weigh up pros and cons, we ask other, totally unqualified, people for their opinions and we think about it too much! We incorrectly assume that success is about age, knowledge, experience, background, money and time. We very quickly talk ourselves in and then back out of pursuing that dream. We then justify why we wouldn't achieve it anyway!

I have been blessed and cursed with the same character trait — act now, think later! This spontaneous and interesting decision-making process has led me to some very expensive lessons:

Interesting decision 1: I spontaneously purchased a part-share in a racehorse.
Lesson: Anything that eats while you sleep is bad for your bank account!

Interesting decision 2: With no experience or idea about hospitality I purchased a café only to find myself two years later in nearly six-figure debt.
Lesson: Some prior research before investing in an industry is a wise idea.

Interesting decision 3: I took and acted on bad advice, not once but two times, from people who really didn't know what they were talking about and I invested in shares. Twice I lost my money.

Lesson: Be very careful who you listen to!

I am happy to say that same fly-by-the-seat-of-my-pants attitude has also provided me with some of the greatest joys in my life, including meeting the person who is now the love of my life, my beautiful wife Laura ...

About six or seven years ago I was killing some time waiting for an appointment and walking through a shopping centre in the city. I walked past a men's fashion store and glanced in — just before I could take the next step, something stopped me. I looked again and I saw the most beautiful girl I had ever seen working behind the counter. I stood there captivated, staring at her but not wanting to get caught I kept looking away, like a naughty school boy. I was frozen; I wanted to go in and talk to her but I was scared that I would embarass myself.

I started to walk away saying, 'Oh well, she wouldn't have been interested in me anyway'. After a couple of steps I stopped myself and said, 'Are you crazy mate? This woman could be the girl of your dreams and you are just going to walk away and never know! You are an idiot — get in there!' So, I then thought to myself, 'I've got nothing to lose, so stop thinking, get some guts and do it'. So, I went in and with knees trembling started talking to this girl. Today Laura is my wife and I am so incredibly grateful that I acted in spite of the fear.

As if that's not amazing enough, I would not be a

successful author today without having made some totally illogical — and unreasonable even — 'accidental' decisions. You will discover, as you read my story, that I was totally unsuited, unqualified and ill-prepared to be an author. Ironically, what seemed to be an accidental, illogical and unreasonable decision has consequently turned my career 180 degrees and led me to live totally aligned with my purpose and passion. Who knew?

I wouldn't change anything for a second and I am truly grateful that thinking (well over-thinking) is not one of my strong points! I am grateful that I am open to the idea of accidental success, even though I believe, beyond doubt, there are no accidents in life. We attract everything that we get — seemingly accidental or not!

I want to share with you the idea that anything is possible for you. I want you to know that if I can achieve in my life what I have, then you can do anything.

As soon as you put this book down you will feel empowered. You will think, *if this bozo can write best selling books then I can do anything!* Read it, enjoy it and use it to build your own belief that you are already good enough to be a best-selling author or achieve whatever you want.

This book has been written for you to use in one or more of three ways:

1. To be a good read and entertain you.

2. To encourage, inspire and empower you to chase your dreams — no matter what they are or how unlikely and out of reach they may seem.

3. To teach you how to write and publish your own best-selling book!

If number one or two are appropriate for you, then enjoy this book. I hope it helps you in your life.

If number three is for you, and it is your dream to be a published author, then at the end of each chapter there is a special section *'Secret author's business ... the steps to success'*. This section is just for you!

Secret author's business ... the steps to success:

This book has been written to encourage you, help you believe in yourself and teach you how to write your own published book(s)! If you are reading this section of the book then I assume you want to be a published author. Believe me when I say, you can do it and it will be one of the best things you will ever do. Most importantly for you right now — it's not as hard as you think.

In this section at the end of each chapter, I will highlight the key questions I had to ask myself and the specific steps and actions I have taken to become a truly passionate and successful best-selling author.

This section will also help you to understand, identify and solve potential challenges. I doubt you will need it but just in case there will be a trouble-shooting section, where appropriate, to help you when you feel lost.

It is my guarantee, that if you follow through on all of these steps, answer all the questions honestly, complete all the activities suggested and be prepared to identify and overcome challenges, then you too will be a best-selling author! Go for it ...

Key questions and actions steps:

1. Are you ready to take the first step?

2. Start reading.

3. Enjoy the journey.

4. Decide to finish what you start!

Chapter One

Born to play sport!

It didn't take too long until I found my place ... It was sport.
In fact, from as early as I can remember I had a ball, a bat,
a racquet or ... my brother in my hands!

I was born a middle child. I am and have always been a classic middle-child, attention–seeking, sooky-la-la mamma's boy and proud of it!

My earliest memory is as a three-year-old whose mother thought was old enough to do without the nappy. Big mistake mum! Just a few minutes later I was running down our long passage way leaving a trail of brown bullets behind me!

I wanted my mum to be proud of me and so I would ask if I could help her with the chores. At that time, and for some reason, ironing seemed like a cool thing to do (I grew out of that pretty quickly!). Mum and dad gave me a mini iron for one of my birthdays and together my mother and I would do the ironing (please keep this secret and really embarassing information under your hat ... thanks!). What a special, new-age, attention-seeking sook I really was!

I always wanted attention. If I didn't get it from my mum, dad, brother, sister or dog I would take matters into my own hands. Feeling unloved, unappreciated and totally into my own self-importance I would grab my pillow, a banana and head off into the big bad world. Crybaby little ol' me was running away! I would run to the deserted laneway down the street and vow never to return. I would set up camp and for the next few days fight off ferocious animals, inclement weather conditions and my own negative thoughts. After endless nights just trying to survive I would finally return home, angry that no-one came to look for me. As I confronted my mother as to why she didn't come to save me, she replied, "You have only been gone 10 minutes!"

It didn't take too long until I found my place. A place where I could get the attention I wanted without risking my life, or so I thought. It was sport. In fact, from as early as I can remember I had a ball, a bat, a racquet or ... my brother in my hands!

I loved kicking the Australian Rules footy with my dad or my brother and if I had no-one to kick the footy with, I played alone kicking a pair of socks around the house pretending to be a champion. I had a hard time explaining to my mum that part of the process of becoming a champion meant that mishaps would occur, such as broken vases caused by flying socks inside the house! When I was old enough I was on a team and playing the sport with passion.

Playing cricket in the hallway and entrance hall with my brother didn't last long — for obvious reasons! Soon we were out in the street playing against our neighbours for the Clonmore Street cup. That also came to an abrupt halt after a ball, that one of us hit, went sailing through the window, smashing the glass and landing too close (for comfort) to my sleeping baby sister.

When I was old enough I was on a team and giving it my all. My clearest memory is of a sunny Saturday when I'd been standing in the field for several hours with no action. Finally a high ball came my way and I sprinted for about 50 metres and then dived, full length, to take the catch of the year. Well, that was the plan anyway. I actually dropped the ball and then got up out of the long grass to find dog sh#@ all over my cricket whites. Hilarious for most (well, almost everyone); tragedy for others (That is, me and my mother. I had to put up with the ridicule and she had to clean the mess).

My mum and dad hated Sundays for one reason — World Championship Wrestling! My brother and I watched and got fired up by the likes of Hulk Hogan, Jesse 'the body' Ventura and George 'the animal' Steele. As soon as it was over I was jumping off the couch onto my brother delivering him with a flying body slam! Then he'd get me into a 'figure 4 leg lock' and needless to say it would end up with something broken and someone in tears — most commonly me (broken and in tears).

I played tennis regularly but, for some reason, never improved. I was really bad at golf — spending most of my time in the bushes, sand or water looking for my ball! I was a very fast runner so had some success sprinting. Playing down-ball against the wall at school during lunchtimes was also a favorite pastime.

It was all about sport!

As I got older and as I realised that I had an affinity with sport, it was decision time. I was good at two main sports, Australian rules football and cricket. I had a decision to make because I couldn't participate fully, to the level I desired, in both of them. One would have to go! I thought for a while about cricket but as I thought about standing out in the field in the middle of a scorching Australian summer for days on end I was leaning towards football. Then I remembered the dog sh#@ on my cricket whites and so it became an easy decision!

So, at the age of about 11 or 12 I realised that my true passion lay with Australian rules football, which then took up most of my thoughts and spare time outside of those things I tried hard but couldn't avoid. I would dream of playing at the highest level. I could see myself running out onto the field in front of thousands of adoring fans and kicking the winning goal. The power of visualising combined with hard work saw me fulfill my dream and play professional football from the age of 17 to 24 years of age.

Secret author's business ... the steps to success:

You are a unique and wonderful person; not perfect, but unique and wonderful! It is important that you find your own place in life, doing the things you love and not comparing yourself to other people. When you approve of and accept yourself for who you are you will find that you are more likely to start achieving the things you desire.

Key questions and actions steps:

1. Make a list of ten of your unique skills, likes and desires.

2. Make a list of ten things you like/love about yourself; no matter how small and insignificant they seem.

3. Make a list of five things you have achieved in life that you are proud of; no matter how small and insignificant they seem.

4. Read each of these lists several times right now and read them each day.

5. You are good enough ... aren't you?

Andrew, the sook!

What a cutie!

Nice outfit! Always after attention.

Mamma's boy ... ironing!

Natural ability ... not!

Chapter Two

Professional football:
Seven years of pain!

*"The pain, the suffering, the discomfort, the frustration,
the humiliation and the abuse were all worth it. Today I can
look back and be proud of what I achieved in my football career
and how it has positively shaped my life and my belief that
I am good enough no matter what."*

Interestingly and ironically I really wasn't the professional footballing type! As I've already explained I was — well, still am actually — a bit of a sook. I was also really skinny, which could be a barrier to professional football; my nicknames ranged from the 'human pipe-cleaner' to the 'chopstick with ears'! My third limitation was probably the most challenging — I just wasn't all that skillful. So, the question must be asked, what drew to me that sport? I can say with great conviction ... I have no idea!

What I knew was I loved the buzz, the adrenaline, the hype and, to be really honest, the thought of fame and girls! I would dream about being a champion and because I had a real act-first-think-later mentality I just had a go at it. It wasn't that I ever really believed I could play professional football. I just didn't know that I couldn't!

In my mind I only had those few small obstacles to overcome: being a sook, being too skinny and having no skill. But rather than focus on my limitations, I focused on my strength — I could run really fast! So that's what I did, just like Forrest Gump, the cry would ring out around the ground, 'Run, Jobbas, Run!' In fact, the big joke was that I would win all of my fights by 50 metres!

As I look back I really don't know how it happened (which you will notice is a common theme running through my life). At the age of 16 I was invited to come and train at the St Kilda Football Club, a professional club in Melbourne, Australia. I truly believe that when you want something bad enough, when you are prepared to work hard with a one-eyed focus and do whatever it takes, you will get there — no matter how unlikely it may seem.

It was a rough introduction to the life of a professional sportsman. Remember I am, by nature, a bit of a sooky-la-la! I was focused on the fame, the fortune and the glamour. I hadn't quite prepared myself for the reality of this life. Ninety per cent of the time over the next seven years is easily summed up in one word — PAIN!

If it wasn't the gut-wrenching pain of training, it was the intense pain of being battered by men much bigger than wimpy little me. If it wasn't the frustrating and soul-destroying pain of missing out on senior selection time and time and time again, it was the humiliating pain of being abused by the coaching staff in front of other players for being 'soft'! If it wasn't the self-esteem lowering pain of being beaten in most of the games we played, it was the unbearable pain of being ridiculed for the entire week after being beaten!

As I look back on those years with a wince I can now see some incredible lessons I learned and the character it helped to shape. Four invaluable lessons come immediately to my mind:

Lesson one: If you get knocked down get up again

I was at the tender age of 17 and weighed a mere 75 kg (165 lbs) when I was selected to play my first senior reserve level game of football with St Kilda Football Club. The opposition players were big, really big, so I was running extra fast that day! My speed came to a grounding halt when I was knocked unconscious by a man who seemed twice my size. I was broken! I was carried off on a stretcher and taken to hospital with severe concussion and a critically damaged ego. I had a choice to make: give up because it is a dangerous game *or* understand that, in the process of any great achievement, I will get knocked down. I am glad I chose to get back up and keep going as that ability has shaped me throughout my life.

Lesson two: Keep showing up

At the age of 18, after two years of working hard with a dream in my heart, I was finally selected to play my very first A-level senior game at St Kilda. It was the last game of the 1983 season. I understandably went into the next pre-season and season excited in anticipation that my successful professional football career was on the verge of exploding. However, that dream was shattered when I started 1984 in the reserve-grade team. I was disappointed but determined to get back into the first-grade side so I kept showing up. From that day, game in and game out, I played harder and better than I had ever played before.

Game in and game out I was passed up for selection. At the halfway mark of the season there was still no sign, despite my exceptionally good form, that I would be selected. I was almost ready to 'throw in the towel' but ... I kept showing up. For the remainder of the 1984 season I missed out on selection every single week. Devastated, I was on the verge of giving up but something inside told me to just keep showing up. The first half of the 1985 season went pretty much the same way, but I stayed resolute to ... just keep showing up! Finally almost two years later I was selected in the first-grade team and from that moment my career was launched. My secret ... I just kept showing up!

Lesson three: Keep moving forward no matter what!

I had made the team, was a regular first-grade player and loving life. I was still a bit bamboozled as to how I actually got there because I really wasn't that skillful. I clearly remember a game when this third lesson was reinforced to me. The following text is the word-for-word commentary by the TV commentators about a particular play on that day:

"... the ball is out to centre wing. Jobling the runner ... he loves to go and off he goes. He bounces the ball badly! And oooh, he handpasses atrociously! But he recovers possession and he kicks it down the ground ... it was good football. He did a few things wrong but recovered it nicely."

I learned a very valuable lesson that day: no matter what mistakes I make or how I may embarrass myself, I just need to keep going and keep moving forward.

Lesson four: You don't always get what you want!

One of the things I always dreamed about as a child, once I had achieved my goal of being a successful professional footballer, was something that most boys hope for. It was having my own football swap card. I could see it in my mind. I would be taking a spectacular mark, kicking a long goal or doing something brilliant. I could visualise it captured on film and forever embossed on a football swap card that all the kids would want to get. Well, that day finally arrived. I got a phone call from a friend telling me that I had my own football swap card. I was so excited, I couldn't wait to see it ... and then I saw it! It wasn't what I had envisioned. It wasn't what I had hoped for. It was a photo that unfortunately captured me doing something I was really good at — falling over! I didn't get what I wanted, but I did achieve something that only a few people ever will and for that I am grateful.

What an amazing seven years it was; the pain, the suffering, the discomfort, the frustration, the humiliation and the abuse were all worth it. Today I can look back and be proud of what I achieved in my football career and how it has positively shaped my life and my belief that I am good enough no matter what.

Secret author's business ... the steps to success:

We have all experienced pain, we have all made mistakes and we have all felt like giving up on things in our life — even you! The goal should never be to try and avoid pain, discomfort, failure or adversity; there is only one place you will ever achieve that and believe me that is not where you want to be!

The secret to success is to embrace and use the discomfort, failures and adversity as lessons to make you better. Look for solutions to overcome them and then enjoy it as you become a stronger, more positively resilient and successful person.

Key questions and actions steps:

1. Describe five different scenarios in which you didn't achieve the outcome you were striving for. Highlight the lesson(s) that you learned from those situations.

2. Think about and describe one or more times in your life when you have experienced discomfort or pain and the amazing benefit that has resulted.

3. In your own words describe how discomfort, pain and resistance will make you stronger and more successful.

Too skinny; run Jobbas, run!

Young and working hard
for the dream.

First senior game, being carried
off unconscious.

More pain!

ANDREW STICKS TO THE TASK

The old axiom that "persistence pays off" has never been more true than in the case of Andrew Jobling who recently earned selection for the senior team after a lengthy stint in the reserves.

A former Beaumaris boy, Andrew is now in his fifth year at St Kilda Football Club. During that time he has been a consistent hard working wingman in firstly the Under 19 team and then the reserve side, but opportunities to show his pacy style in senior company have been rare.

He first tasted the big-time in the final round of 1983 when he was selected on the interchange bench against Collingwood. He experienced the traditional welcome of the Victoria Park crowd when he was loudly abused as he warmed up inside the boundary line. Andrew kept plugging away in the reserves throughout 1984, but could not break into the senior twenty. It would have been easy to fall into despondency, but Andrew never lost his faith that he would eventually make the grade and the writing was on the wall when he was chosen in the squad of twenty three players for a match earlier this year. "The Age" remarked at the time that he would be making his debut, obviously unaware that he had played that solitary game in 1983. As it turned out Andrew was not in the final twenty against Fitzroy that day, but several commentators with a less than keen eye for detail called his name instead of Andrew Manning who wore Jobling's jumper when his own was torn.

A fortnight ago Andrew Jobling actually did return to the senior team against Melbourne, and "The Age", not content with making a mistake once, said that he was ready to make his senior debut.

Many people who view the reserve games each week believe that he should have returned to the senior squad much earlier, but Andrew himself is not bitter and says "having played that many games in the reserves gives me a lot of experience as a basis to work on."

Andrew, a third year Phys Ed Student at Rusden College, has played as a defender in all of the reserves games this year and it was in that capacity that he was selected against Melbourne at VFL Park. When it was suggested that VFL Park on a rainy, slippery day was not the ideal place to press your claims for a regular senior position Andrew gave a surprising reply.

"It was good to play at VFL Park because there is plenty of room in which you can run to space and create the play. On many of the other grounds you are cramped for room."

It is obvious that 20 year old Andrew thinks hard about his game and we are certain that he will make his mark . . . even upon forgetful newspaper reporters!

Keep showing up!

SAINTS
ANDREW JOBLING
ST. KILDA   114 of 132

SCANLENS

*The footy card ...
falling over!*

*At the bottom
of the pack.*

Essendon's Mark Harvey hangs onto a mark at Moorabbin yesterday despite the attentions of St Kilda's Silvio Foschini. Saint Andrew Jobling found himself at the bottom as did Essendon defender Paul Weston. Picture: RUSSELL WHELAN.

Working hard.

The dream realised.

The dream realised.

St Kilda youngster Andrew Jobling . . . a strong will to succeed.

Jobling's on the job

By JON ANDERSON

IN these days of VFL clubs constantly trying to entice reluctant interstate stars to play in Melbourne, it's a refreshing change to meet a local who desperately wants to make the grade here.

And for St. Kilda youngster Andrew Jobling, just playing at senior level in the VFL is a dream come true.

Ever since the 20-year-old defender can remember, he has had his sights set on making it at the highest level.

After five years of battling in the Under 19s and Reserves, Jobling has shown in four senior games this year that he might fit into a rare group in the VFL — those who play better at senior level than in the Reserves.

His pace and courage were never in doubt, according to St. Kilda general manager Ian Stewart, but few of the good judges at Moorabbin thought Jobling would succeed in the firsts.

However, succeed he has, as a half-back and a back pocket. Originally a wingman, fresh-faced Andrew doesn't mind where he plays as long as it's in the St. Kilda senior team.

"Just say I'm rapt, really happy or whatever you like," said Jobling this week from Rusden College, where he's enrolled as a third year physical education student.

"Sure I became frustrated and depressed playing in the Reserves all the time but I really believed one day I'd make it.

"Now that I have, I don't intend giving it away."

Jobling was born in Beaumaris and played with his local side in the Under 17s after spending his junior years at Cheltenham Park.

It's probably his determination which got him where he is now while less fair dinkum players have given it away.

"When you work so hard for something, it becomes a big goal and it's no use throwing it in," he said.

Jobling, along with Saint youngsters Andrew Manning, Ben Ingleton and David Grant, has provided his team with something to work on in the future.

Stewart believes this quartet and others such as Tony Lockett, Paul Temay and Danny Frawley will see St Kilda become a competitive unit in 1985.

The glamour.

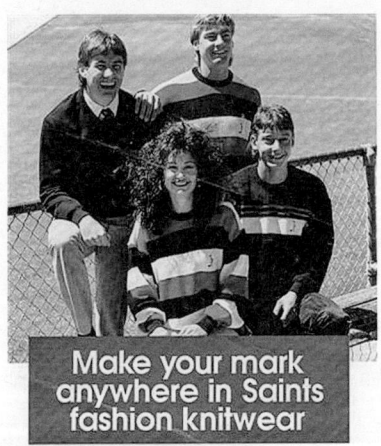

A model I ain't!

Chapter Three

For all the wrong reasons

"This teaching career I had fallen into for all the wrong reasons had helped me to realise exactly what I did and didn't want for my career and it only took four years. I was a slow learner but at least I was a learner!"

This pre-occupation with sport and football — actually a better word would be obsession with football — meant that other things were forced way down on the priority list. Little insignificant things, at that time, like school, study, reading and education. I never gave them much thought because I was going to be a professional footballer so I didn't need it! But I did have to go to school as my parents were paying a lot of money for my education. I had a work ethic and I did have enough pride in myself that I didn't want to fail.

So, I scraped through school on the bare minimum of effort with English my worst subject by far. In fact the only reason I passed English in Year 12 was because I received some tutoring from my mum's best friend and colleague who was the head of English at the same private school at which my mum worked in Melbourne. This lovely lady, who was also on the Year 12 English examination board, gave me a few friendly and well-directed pointers just at the right time of the year! Phew!

So again, somehow, I finally scraped through secondary school. Then the next step ... oh no, now I had to think about tertiary education. What was I going to do? I was 18 years old and didn't really care, as long as it had something to do with sport! After rejecting ninety-nine per cent of suggestions from my parents, I finally decided on a Physical Education degree. Why? Because it sounded like sport to me!

All by accident, it was the perfect choice and I loved this course. Well the first two years anyway as I got to do the things I loved most — play sport, chase girls and have fun! Sure there was a bit of study involved, but I didn't want to overdo it and burn myself out. I really enjoyed learning about different sports: basketball, netball, badminton, gymnastics, hockey, lacrosse, just to name a few.

I even got excited about ballet because I learned how to *assemblé, changement de pieds* and of course *plié*. One of my favorite party tricks, which impressed the girls and often got me punched by the boys, was my interpretation of a classical ballet routine ... *assemblé, assemblé, changement*!

I was young, I was dumb, I was having fun and I wasn't too concerned about the consequences of my actions — clearly! I remember one day in first or second year, I was in a gymnastics class watching my teacher performing an impressive routine on the parallel bars. He was a former Australian Olympic gymnast, so you would have thought I would be impressed and interested to learn from him. But, no, I was way to into myself and being the centre of attention!

He was videoing his routine so we could watch it and learn from it at a later time. So 'dumb-and-dumber' me decided to become the star attraction. I positioned myself in front of the camera but behind my teacher. I turned around, back to the camera, pulled down my pants, bent over and 'smiled' to the camera, much to everyone's amusement — except my teachers!

As he was watching his performance on playback I decided the smartest and safest thing for me to do would be to disappear to the farthest corner of the gym. From behind a stack of crash mats I watched from a distance and saw him shake his head. I found out later what he said as he was watching my unique performance, "Some people grow up, others just grow old!"

So, as you can see I was enjoying my course without really any idea of where it was leading me and, to be honest at that time of my life, I didn't really care! Then in the third year of this four-year course I got a rude awakening as I was told I had to arrange practice teaching rounds. I didn't understand why and so I went and asked the question. Well, it seemed and was explained to me that I was doing a four-year bachelor of education degree, which was a teaching degree. How about that? I was going to be a teacher. Who knew?

It took me a short while to process this new information. Me? A teacher? I couldn't quite get my head around it. Actually, on reflection, it was quite ironic. I was not interested in study, just sport. I was not a reader or even really that interested in learning. But here I was heading into a teaching career for all the wrong reasons. Well, I soon just decided, with the 'fly-by-the-seat-of-my-pants' attitude I lived by to just go with it and that's what I did. I became a teacher — by accident!

After somehow successfully completing four years of tertiary education I vowed that reading was no longer a necessity in my life and I would give it up. Except, of course, for the essentials: the sport section of the newspaper and comic books! Sure I was going to be a teacher, but I didn't need to read — that was for the students!

As you have probably already guessed, my teaching career didn't last that long. I taught for four years, which was long enough for me to realise I'd found a true passion for helping, educating and inspiring others. However, the challenge I had with teaching teenagers was that most of them didn't want to be helped, educated or inspired by me. So, most of my time was spent trying to get them to just listen to me! I thought I had better get out quickly before I strangled one of them. (Please note: I would never actually strangle a teenager!)

This teaching career I had fallen into for all the wrong reasons had helped me to realise exactly what I did and didn't want for my career and it only took four years. I was a slow learner but at least I was a learner!

I decided it was time to take a slightly more calculated approach to my career. The throwing-mud-against-the-wall-and-hoping-for-the-best approach had got me only so far but so far in the wrong direction! As I transitioned out of teaching I decided to get back to and stick with my passion, so that is exactly what I did ...

Secret author's business ... the steps to success:

There are times in life we make decisions for the wrong reasons. There are two different scenarios where this is the case:

1. Decisions made for us by other people: parents, teachers, friends, etc. They are often made with the best intentions but are not the right decisions for us. My parents tried very hard to guide me down a certain path of study which, for them, seemed to be good advice for parents to give their teenage son, but which was totally wrong for me.

2. Decisions we make that seem to defy all logic and reason. We often don't even understand why we are making the decision as it is an intuitive 'gut' feeling. Something we get in our head and heart and we can't be dissuaded from that path.

I have always gone with option two and I will tell you, in every case, it has led me to lessons that I needed to learn and/or places I didn't even realise I wanted to arrive. My advice to you is to go with your intuition, no matter how illogical it may seem as it will always lead you where you want to be.

Key questions and actions steps:

1. Describe a time you went with your 'gut' to make a seemingly illogical decision and the results that were achieved as a result.

2. Remove all logic and reasoning from your thoughts right now and describe the one thing, deep in your heart, that you would like to achieve.

3. In regards to that one thing, answer this question honestly — is what you are currently doing going to lead you to achieve it?

Chapter Four

Time to Change

"No-one likes to change, but everyone likes the result of change."

I left my teaching job with mixed emotions — joy and happiness! With even more joy and happiness I moved into the next career phase of my life which was the fitness industry. I became a gym manager for a short time and then moved into personal training. I loved it! It was pay back! I thought back to all the pain and suffering I had been subjected to as a professional footballer by the heartless fitness trainers and I thought, now is my turn to inflict some pain! I gave my clients pain and then they paid me. It was like a double-bonus!

In all seriousness, the reality was that training hard was all I knew. In my mid-twenties when I started personal training, I had just come out of my seven-year career as a professional footballer. For all of those seven years I had been indoctrinated with the attitude and mentality of 'no-pain-no-gain', 'all-or-nothing' and 'go-hard-or-go-home'. During my professional football career we climbed cliffs and ran up mountains. We carried logs and tractor tyres. We ran more 400 metre sprints than I care to remember. As I have already mentioned I was in pain for most of those seven years. We were yelled at, abused, told we were weak and instructed to just toughen up. I knew nothing more than to train hard until I felt like passing out and there were times when I did!

So as I began my personal training career this is all I knew about training. I trained my clients like I was used to training and being trained myself — with no mercy! If they could walk out after a training session I felt like I had let them down. If they vomited, I thought it was their way of saying 'thank you!'

Again I am sure you can imagine I was not having a lot of success in the early days of my personal trainer career! As much as I was enjoying myself, my clients were getting injured, not getting results, cancelling regularly and even not showing up at all. My initial thought was that they were soft, weak and they needed to toughen up. But after some reflection I realised the problem — I was an idiot!

Maybe 'idiot' is too strong a word — the reality was that I didn't know what I didn't know. I was under the mistaken impression, as a result of my experiences, that the secret to being healthy, lean and happy was exercise. I simply and naively thought that if you trained often enough, long enough and hard enough you could achieve any result you wanted. In this conclusion however, I failed to take into account two important considerations. The first was the power of food and good nutrition in this whole process. The second, and maybe more critical, was that most people don't want to be professional athletes! They just want to be fitter, leaner and healthier.

It was time for some soul searching. I really had to challenge the way I had done things for so long. Looking back I am astounded at the lack of nutritional education and resources at the St Kilda Football Club in the 1980s — supposedly a professional club. There was no-one there with any idea about some of the most critical elements of success: good nutrition and recovery. I remember players drinking alcohol on a Friday night before a game and even players smoking cigarettes straight after a game!

I cannot remember one time when we were sat down with a qualified dietician or sports nutritionist to help us put together an eating plan specific to the rigors of professional sport. I can't remember one time when we were encouraged to drink water — even on the hottest and most dehydrating days. I cannot remember easy sessions where we could just let our aching muscles renew, recover and regenerate.

Therefore, for me to change my thinking from a pre-conditioned hardcore, all-or-nothing approach to one which promoted balance and enjoyment was a difficult shift for me. I remember clearly, after I decided to place more importance on nutrition, throwing myself into some intense learning about the power of food. I actually read some books (even though I vowed that I would never read again)! I researched, I learned, I experimented and I developed an eating plan for myself that many people would call extreme just like my training regime.

I decided if I was going to do it I would do it properly, so I went hardcore! I gave up sugar, chocolate, desserts, fatty foods and I ate fruits, vegetables and lean proteins. I became one of those really painful people. You know the ones you hate to go out with? I would examine menus with a fine tooth comb and reject or accept restaurants and cafés based on this analysis. I then changed every order. I ordered salad with the dressing on the side, no sauces on my food and I tried to modify every meal on the menu to suit my extreme eating standards. Boy was it stressful!

Then if that wasn't stupid enough, I tried to make my clients eat the same way! Yep, I was really that dumb! They still kept cancelling, but now, when they did show up, they would also just conveniently forget their food diaries to avoid the wrath of their psycho trainer (me) who would berate them for eating the most miniscule amount of chocolate!

I am obviously a slow learner but in my desire to be better at what I do and to make a difference in the lives of more people it was a necessity. No-one likes to change, but everyone likes the result of change so eventually I did get it. One day, one step and one meal at a time I finally learned the concept of balance, moderation and enjoyment. Not only that, but I developed a simple eating formula that was getting results and working for me and my clients.

Now, all that was left was to get my message out to the masses but how could I do that?

Secret author's business ... the steps to success:

To be successful in life, you need to be able to make course corrections along the way. You need to know when you are veering off course and make the right changes at the right times. If you don't make any changes you will end up where you are heading! I hope it is where you want to arrive.

Most people just keep doing what they are doing, whether they love it or not, and often end up at a place regretting they didn't make changes earlier in their lives. Don't make that mistake. Make the changes you need to make now.

Key questions and actions steps:

1. Is what you are doing leading you to the place you ultimately want to be?

2. Deep down you know what you need to change don't you. What is it?

3. What small change can you make today to move you back on the path that leads to your desired destination?

Chapter Five

Here I go again!

"I made a decision. Not a smart decision, but a decision nevertheless! Interestingly what I have found to be true in my life is that any decision — even a poorly considered one — is better than no decision at all!"

I was excited. I took my newly acquired knowledge and thought about how I could best share it with the world. I'm a big picture thinker and I'm a doer. I'm certainly *not* an analyser, nor am I very logical or sensible. I wanted to change the world. I wanted to get my message out there to make the world a happier and healthier place.

Consequently, I made a decision of how I would do it. Not a smart decision, but a decision nevertheless! Interestingly what I have found to be true in my life is that any decision — even a poorly considered one — is better than no decision at all! And, most importantly, it got me into action.

I had learned a lot about good nutrition, I loved eating and I wanted to bring healthy food to 'the people'. So logically, in my mind, buying a café was just a natural choice. Okay, so I knew nothing about the hospitality industry but surely I could learn. Of course I was already a part-owner of a personal training business and working

70–80 hours per week ... but surely there is always more time to be found!

I was passionate about helping people with their health through good nutrition. I got the idea in my head that I would own and run a successful café and no-one could dissuade me from my path. A path of destruction and then valuable lessons as it turned out!

My plans were grand, my action was swift but my preparation left much to be desired. I wanted to provide high quality natural and healthy meals. I wanted to offer education through seminars and newsletters. I wanted to provide a fully personalised meal and home delivery service. I was focused, I was excited, I was passionate and so I charged ahead.

The café was fresh and new. I was initially incredibly excited about and focused on a successful venture. I then did what I had set out to do and provided the very best fresh and natural ingredients in all of the meals. I ran regular seminars to add value and to educate and empower anyone interested in better health and wellbeing.

We then set up a wonderful meal service specifically designed for and targeted at time-poor professionals. We prepared their meals, we delivered their meals and we made a difference in their lives. What we didn't do was allow for expansion and growth — the system was not scalable. The more clients we got the more labour intensive and expensive the process became! We started making silly mistakes, we began falling behind on orders and deliveries, and consequently the quality of our service declined.

Then if that wasn't bad enough, one year in and just as the café was starting to do well, another café opened two doors away. They offered lower quality meals with less healthy ingredients and a cheaper price-tag. All of a sudden our wonderfully regular and loyal clients started to migrate to the dark side! All about price! It was about this time I started to wonder, *what the @#$%&! am I doing?*

My 70–80 hour a week personal training business quickly ballooned into 100–120 hours working seven days a week in the two businesses. One business was filling my bank and the other emptying it just as quickly!

My vision was to teach, inspire and serve people through my café. What I didn't understand, at the time, was that running a successful café required doing many things I wasn't passionate about at all like bookkeeping, accounting, payroll, permits, rules and regulations! Not to mention cleaning dirty pots, pans, dishes, floors and dealing with unreliable staff and cranky chefs! I am a creative person, someone who loves making a difference and acting spontaneously — as you have discovered — my strengths are certainly not those other things.

So have a guess how I spent most of the time in my business? I spent most of my time working on my weaknesses. I invested valuable time and energy learning to keep the books, track the money and all the stuff that, quite honestly, left me stressed, empty and unfulfilled. I also had to often help cleaning, scrubbing and mopping. I spent less and less time doing the things I loved. Consequently the business started going backwards financially, erroneously leading me to believe I needed to spend even more time doing the stuff I hated. Two years later, stressed and exhausted, I sold the business at a massive loss.

Ironically, in my desire to force myself to do things

that were opposed to my natural character and instincts, and learn all aspects of the business to save money, I found myself in close to a six-figure debt. Hindsight is a wonderful thing. All I had to do was find someone who was good at and enjoyed the things I didn't. It would have allowed me to focus my time on my strengths, my passion and creating my vision. Who knows where that business might be today?

This whole process and experience of taking action, owning a café and basically working myself and my bank account into the ground left me disillusioned, deflated, discouraged and exhausted. I couldn't quite understand what I was doing wrong. I was just doing what I had always been taught — working hard!

Then I did something totally against my nature; I decided to start reading!

Secret author's business ... the steps to success:

You may have heard about 'paralysis by analysis'. It is not something I have ever suffered from! On the contrary, my affliction is and has always been 'act now think about consequences later'. As you have already read to this point in my story, I have made decisions that have led to some very expensive lessons but, just so you know, I wouldn't change them for anything.

I have always said that I would much rather live with the pain of acting spontaneously and experiencing some discomfort and very expensive lessons, than be haunted by the regret I would feel if I never tried. I have never been one to over-think, analyse or weigh up pros and cons and so many of my decisions to act were made in haste and led to seemingly undesirable consequences. On reflection every decision to act, no matter how illogical or spontaneous they were at the time, has taught me, shaped me and positioned me to be right now where I am in my life. That is exactly where I want to be.

I want to encourage you to think less and act more. That doesn't necessarily mean make ill-considered decisions. It means stop letting doubts and over analysis determine your future. Be known as someone who takes action and who learns from experience. Don't be scared to try and fail — be much more scared of never trying!

Key questions and actions steps:

1. Describe a time when you acted spontaneously. What was the result? What was the achievement or what was the lesson?

2. What are you procrastinating on at the moment? Is it starting to write your book?

3. What is the worst thing that would happen if you just decided to take action and get started today? Could you live with that?

4. What is the best thing that would happen if you just decided to take action and get started today? Is it worth it?

5. Make a decision and take action on something ... anything ... right now!

Chapter Six

A light bulb moment: The power of the written word

"When I started reading I quickly realised there was a significant difference between reading the words and listening to them."

As you may have already gathered I am, and have always been, an action type of person. Always looking for the next adventure, the next challenge, the next activity. For much of my life the thought of sitting in the same place for long enough to read was not something I could relate to or was inclined to do. The only reading I really did, as a child, was the reading I had to do, boring school books! I would last about five minutes and then either fall asleep or put the book down and be out kicking the footy. I just couldn't see the benefit or how reading could help me achieve what I wanted in my life — so I didn't do it!

I never really understood how reading could or would possibly change my life until I actually started doing it, and doing it with the right heart. As I mentioned, I read through school because I had to, not because I wanted to. After I finished my tertiary education I thought that I didn't need (and wouldn't have to) read anymore. I believed it just took up time that could be used far more effectively kicking a footy, having fun or watching TV. To be fair on myself, I did read between the ages of 23 and 38. I read the sport section of the newspaper and comics! What a literary genius I was.

Through forcing myself to read to find out more about nutrition, something amazing started to happen. I actually learned some things. What a crazy concept! I didn't read much and I certainly didn't read for long as I would predictably be asleep within 10 minutes, which was the unfortunate legacy of a 15-hour work day. Even so, in these short sessions of reading I learned more than I had learned through all of my previous years of education.

When I actually started this reading at the age of 38 my world started to change. Today my life is unrecognisable from the one I was living back then. I love every second of my life today. You might ask, "All this from reading?" My answer is a resounding, "Yes!"

It truly was a light-bulb moment for me. I started to regret that I wasn't open to finding this out earlier in my life but I just didn't know what I didn't know. Actually when I think about it, I am sure many of my teachers had tried to explain it to me, but I didn't want to listen. I was going to a footballer. No brains required! Let me share something that I have learned — reading will change your life just as it has mine.

I pretty quickly realised there is a major difference between reading and listening. For most of my life I had been listening to people telling and teaching me. That was always easier! It was easier to listen to something or someone than to read. I listened to people, to CDs, to TV to a range of audio programs but nothing ever significantly changed in my life. When I started reading I quickly realised there was a significant difference between reading the words and listening to them. Listening didn't have the same profound impact as reading the words to myself.

Like most of us, I am busy in my head. That voice in there is always on the go and talking 24/7, whether I am awake or asleep. This inner voice of mine is constantly chattering and making judgments. It is telling me, 'I can' or 'I can't', 'I like it' or 'I don't'. This internal voice is determining what I achieve in my life. I started to become aware that as I listened to something, either someone else talking, the TV, an audio book or at a seminar, my little inner voice was talking all the way through. How rude!

I was putting my own, often incorrect, spin on what I was listening to. I sometimes disagreed with what was being said. I was, at times, scared of what was being said. But most of the time I wasn't even focused on what was being said because I was distracting myself with my own noise. No matter how good the information I only did what I told myself to do — not what I was being encouraged to do.

When I started reading that inner negative voice amazingly stopped! Why? Because, whilst reading, I was speaking to myself. All of a sudden the words in the book became my inner voice; I was taking those profound, inspiring, empowering and informative words off the page and depositing them firmly into my head! Like magic I could instantly control my self-talk through reading. Instead, it was my own voice telling me stuff that would improve my knowledge and improve my life. When I started reading I started achieving more things in my life because I was now reading words and telling myself that I could be successful. I was being inspired by new ideas, different perspectives and stories of others who had achieved great things.

One word, one page and one book at a time I started to read and talk to myself about what was possible for me. Over time I started to believe it and, surprise, surprise, it actually started to happen in my life.

Let me give you an example. Through all of my years in the health and fitness area I believed that the secret to a long and happy life came down to eating well and exercising regularly. I am sure you would agree that this is a very common belief. Well, I was reading a book called *The Magic is in the Extra Mile*, by Larry Di Angi, and I read three paragraphs that forever changed my thinking, my approach to life and my impact on other people.

It read:

A national news program conducted a study of fifty people who have lived over 100 years and still lead active, happy lives. The researchers specifically looked for similarities in diet, exercise, lifestyle and habits that could contribute to their longevity and quality of life. What they found was amazing.

We are becoming more and more aware of the great benefits of a healthy diet and exercise, and the researchers expected to find these factors to be the major contributors. Through an extensive interviewing process, the news team found that some of the participants in this study had what would be considered good diets. An equal number of people were not as healthy in their food choices. Exercise and other areas of lifestyle were also not found to be a common thread throughout the group.

However, two things were overwhelmingly consistent among over 90% of those studied. What were these consistent traits? Nine out of ten said that throughout their entire lives they awoke every morning with an **attitude of gratitude** for one more day of life and they **saw each day as a precious gift**. Secondly, nine out of ten stated that they felt that life **was too short to hold grudges or spend time complaining**, and **they forgave people quickly** and **refused to dwell on negative thoughts**.

Wow, what a paradigm shifter! It helped to answer some of those questions I often asked like: *why are there so many people who are so fit and healthy who get sick or die before their time?* It also answers a question for me about my great-grandmother. Until that point I was always baffled about how she could smoke like a chimney, drink brandy every day and go on to live an active fulfilling life well into her nineties. I suddenly understood that our lives are a total package and, of course we need to eat well and exercise regularly, but we need to be happy, grateful and learn how to live in the moment. Powerful stuff!

It was hard to believe that reading just 218 words would have such a profound impact on someone. I then wondered how many people's lives were positively impacted after reading that very same piece of writing.

Then to compound this understanding about the power of the written word even more, my mum showed me a letter she received from her grandmother. This original letter was typed by my Hungarian great-grandmother and sent to my mother in 1941 for her sixth birthday, just two years after my mum and her parents had come to Australia from Hungary. When my mother received this letter she was experiencing challenging times coming to terms with her new life. She kept it with her for more than 60 years!

My dear, sweet, little Susy. I will wright to You, in English for I want you shall understand every word of my letter, I hope it will arrive intime, to your birhday. I send you my angel, thousand, and thousen kisses, and I am so sorry not to bee by You and not kiss You with the greatest love on this day. Now You are 6, year old, an adult young girl, who is going to scool, and klearning and behaving himself surely very good, and who also helping at his parents, in the shop, and also in the household. But I hope You d,ont forget, to play much with your little friends, you send in a letter some nice words to us, that You are learning about the good god in school. Please pray to Him every evening, before going sleeping, that he shall help us, to come aut to you, and then I w never will be sorry, and we would learn together, but also play, and take walk and swimming in the sea, would,nt it bee wonderfull? It will come to You a hungarian young man, who will bring you a little brslet of gold, with a heart, and another joujou, it is the birthday present of the two grandmother, györi gyösi and lellei. Wear it, in health, and shall brin you fortune my dear. Next You must personelly, describe me, what did you got for X.mas, and how di did you celebrated, the birthday, of your Daddy, and yours, and by did cooked Your mammy, and how do you like uncle Andrew, an your aunty Elisabeth.
I embrace, you with the greatest love. so many time, that you will be unable to cont it.

Your

lellei nagymama.

Bpest. 1941. jan. 11.

The letter to my mother from her grandmother.

My mum read this letter when she needed reassurance that she was loved. She read it when she doubted herself. She read it when she just wanted to feel good. I have no idea how many times she read that one untidy piece of writing over 60 years ... but what I do know is it made a profound difference in her life.

Hmmm ... there is something in this reading and book thing!

Secret author's business ... the steps to success:

When I finally understood the power of the written word and I really immersed myself into reading, my life started to improve dramatically. I started to think differently, act differently and as a result I began to get different results.

If you want to be the best author you can be and write the most compelling, entertaining, inspiring and/or informative book possible, then you need to have no doubt in your mind about the power of the written word and the positive impact your book will have on the reader. When you have that clarity you are ready to get started.

Key questions and actions steps:

1. What is it about reading that you get the most out of?

2. What has positively changed in your life as a result of reading?

3. How will your book change lives?

4. Choose one of your favorite books and write:
    a. the title and author,
    b. what impacted you the most about the book, and
    c. a personal testimonial to the author (and, if you feel the urge, actually send it).

Chapter Seven

An unreasonable and illogical decision

"When I cast my mind back to that decision I am incredibly grateful I didn't think about it too much. Why? Because it was a totally unreasonable decision for me to make and if I had thought about it for even a second, there is no doubt I would have talked myself out of it."

The writing was on the wall, my café was failing miserably and I knew it. I was working harder than ever to save it. Looking back now I can see that all I was doing, in my obsessive ignorance, was akin to re-shuffling deck chairs on the Titanic.

Despite the café's downward spiral, I still had a burning passion and desire to spread the message about good nutrition. I would talk about my ideas with many people, who would often ask me if there were any good books on the subject. I thought about it and finally came to the conclusion that there were lots of great books but none that were user-friendly for most people.

All the books I had read about nutrition suggested, promoted or discussed methods that required some kind of complicated or extreme approach. Such as don't eat carbohydrates after 3pm, don't combine protein and carbohydrates, eat fruit only before midday, no carbohydrates at all, count calories, weigh this and measure that and be careful of your blood type, etc.

Now I am not saying these books are wrong or bad. What I am saying is that, for many people, they are too hard to implement and maintain and most people will never stick at them long enough to get results. They often weren't realistic or lifestyle-friendly books.

Then it came out of no-where ... another brainwave!

At the point in my life when I was working 100 plus hours, seven days per week in my own personal training business and a failing café I officially made the most illogical decision I have ever made. With my new-found appreciation of the written word, I decided I was going to write a book!

When I cast my mind back to that decision I am incredibly grateful I didn't think about it too much. Why? Because it was a totally unreasonable decision for me to make and if I had thought about it for even a minute, there is no doubt I would have talked myself out of it. I was already working 12–15 hour days, seven days per week. I had a failing café that required my full attention. I was a footballer and a personal trainer who for most of my life vowed I would not read any more books other than comics or the sport section of the newspaper. I only just passed English in Year 12. Who possibly would or could have connected Andrew Jobling with the word 'author'. It just did not compute!

So, in my ignorance, naivety and without asking anyone else what they thought about the idea, I just started writing. I remember the day clearly. I was at the café, in the back office and staring at the bank balance hoping that by some miracle money would just start appearing. I can't tell you exactly what I was thinking — clearly! I have a feeling I was just looking for a distraction from my harsh reality. So I simply sat down and started planning my book.

I had no idea what I was doing or really how I was going to get it done. All I knew was this is how I would get my message out, that this book would be written and that it would make a difference in the life of others. I remembered the lesson I learned from my football days. That is, when you know what you want, why you want it and if you want it badly enough then you will always work out how to get it done. No matter how unlikely it may seem. I just went into forward motion!

I really don't understand why, with everything I had going on in my life, I was so determined to become an author. I honestly can't remember the thought process that led me to the decision, but I can remember the feelings I experienced.

Initially I felt intense excitement — the excitement we all feel at the beginning of a new journey and the anticipation of an amazing outcome. The next feeling that came pretty quickly was fear! Fear of the unknown. Fear that I couldn't do it. Fear of other people's opinions. Fear about the process. Fear of my ignorance. Fear of making another poor decision. But, again, the main overwhelming feeling I experienced at that time was a burning desire!

Logically I knew I could write the book. I could write and speak so it made sense. I knew I had the persistence and discipline to 'keep showing up' and get it finished which was a character trait I had developed through my professional football career. So, logically I knew I could write a book. It was a mechanical function and a simple process to get the job done.

However, I had learned a long time ago that ability, knowledge and awareness were not enough to ensure I would actually finish this book. I had to think more deeply. The question I had to ask myself was not, 'Do I want to write a book?' the key question was, 'Why do I want to write a book?'

Let's face it a book is just a heap of pages with words on it and is only of benefit to someone who reads it and acts on the information. The main reason I wanted to write this book was to empower people to take action and take control of their wellbeing, and hence their lives. This thought got me incredibly excited. If I could make a global difference in the lives of other people it would be a dream come true.

Then when I stopped to think about it, I realised there were many other powerful reasons which led me into this seemingly illogical action. I wanted to make money! Tacky maybe, but I was sick of working stupid hours and then going broke. I desperately wanted to create multiple income streams to give me choices about what I could buy and how I could spend my time. I wanted to develop my speaking career to become a professional speaker. At one stage I was told by a speaker agent, in no uncertain terms, to write a book and not to come back until it was done and published!

I wanted my family and friends to be proud of me; I wanted to encourage and inspire them, through my actions, to follow their own dreams. I wanted credibility and to be respected in the industry in which I had spent so many years of my life. Finally, something that has motivated me throughout my life, I wanted to achieve something that only a small minority of people will ever achieve. On the back of my business card is the quote, 'I will do today what others won't so I can live tomorrow like others can't.'

In my heart I was ready to write this book; now I just had to deal with a small thing called belief!

Secret author's business ... the steps to success:

It may seem unlikely and there may seem to be many challenges, barriers and obstacles to prevent you from achieving your dream of being a published author. But, as you will know from previous achievements, if you are clear on what you want and the desire is strong enough to achieve it then you will always find a way to get the result.

Before launching into the writing process, there are some foundational steps that must be taken to ensure you mentally and emotionally prepare yourself to finish what you start. Most people are great at starting things, but only a tiny percentage will ever see them through to a successful completion as they let life, other people and excuses stop them. They were simply not prepared for success.

Just to put this into perspective for you, I would say that there are many people in the world who would like to write a book. Out of these people, probably no more than one or two per cent of them will actually start the process. Out of these people who decide to become an author, only three to five per cent of them will end up with a published book! When anyone can, but only such a tiny percentage of people actually do, I had to ask why?

I share these numbers to excite you, not depress you because I now know what it takes to be one of the successful few — and I am about to share it with you. You see, out of everyone who sets out to be an author and decides categorically to *finish what they start*, 100 per cent of them will be successful.

Those who made a firm decision and got the job done all had clarity in two key areas. They had a dream (i.e. they knew *what* they wanted) and a burning desire (i.e. they knew *why* they wanted it). Most people start with the dream to write a book, but they don't finish the job because they haven't connected it emotionally to what is most important in their lives. The result is that they get knocked off course by a number of things, which they will continue to justify until their dying day.

For you to write and publish your book not only do you need to know *what* it looks like (the dream), but you need to powerfully and emotionally connect it with all the compelling reasons *why* it must be done (the desire). Once this connection has been made and the desire is strong enough then you will automatically make a powerful, non-negotiable decision to get it done. Decision (it will happen!) = Dream (what?) + Desire (why?)!

The following activities are the critical foundation to prepare you for success.

Key questions and actions steps:

1. Think about the testimonial you wrote in the previous chapter for the author of your favorite book. How would you feel if you received something like that? Write yourself a testimonial! Write it as if it is written from someone else to you about the impact your book has had on their life.

2. Why is it important for you to write this book? List 5–10 reasons.

3. What would be the consequences if you didn't get it done? Would that bother you?

4. Describe in writing how your published book will positively impact each of the following eight areas of your life:
   a. self,
   b. relationships,
   c. career,
   d. financial,
   e. wellbeing,
   f. lifestyle,
   g. social, and
   h. spiritual/contribution.

5. Answer the following questions:
   a. What is the theme and/or concept of your book?
   b. Who is your target audience?
   c. What immediate impact do you want the book to have on others?
   d. What is the long-term result you want the book to produce for the reader?
   e. What do you want them to say about the book?
   f. What is your idea of the title? Is it catchy, will it get attention and does it grasp the essence of your book?

6. Read all of these answers to yourself on a regular basis to keep you focused, on-track, connected and committed to the end result.

7. Is your dream and desire strong enough for you to keep going, no matter the circumstances, to be a published author?

Chapter Eight

Belief is an inside job!

"I repeated those positive statements and each day I believed a little bit more and grew more confident in my ability. Eventually I knew deep in my heart that I was going to be a published author."

Using my own version of logic I knew I could easily be an author. The problem, in my experience, is that logic very rarely has anything to do with it! On the surface the challenges I had to contend with seemed solvable, yet there was an underlying anxiety that I needed to explore.

My first major obstacle was my belief in my ability to be an author, as clearly the odds were stacked against me. But I reasoned that if I can speak and communicate verbally and with clarity then I can write so that people can understand.

Secondly, the thought of what it would take to write a whole book was pretty daunting — but then I asked myself, 'What is a book?' It is just a group of words strung into a sentence, a whole heap of sentences that form a paragraph, lots of paragraphs to make up a chapter and a handful of chapters that create a book. Simple! So really, a book is written *just one word at a time*. So, I thought to myself, 'I can do that!'

The last obvious hurdle I could see was finding the time to fit writing into my crazy life as I was already working 100 plus hours per week. I did need to eat and sleep, but I decided that TV was not essential in my life, so I could do without it for a period of time. Along with that there were some other small things I knew I could cut out which would enable me to find small regular pockets of time.

Logically and on the surface it looked simple and do-able, but what was bubbling away under the surface? From past experience I knew my self-talk and deep-down belief in my ability would determine my results. It really had nothing to do with logic. What I was saying to myself, consciously and unconsciously, on an ongoing basis would guide my actions, good or bad. So regardless of logic, I had to examine any negative self-talk and limiting beliefs which would stop me from achieving this powerful dream.

In addition to the feeling of excitement about this new journey, I could feel an underlying anxiety running through my body. Why? The anxiety could only come from a belief or a thought that is in conflict with what I wanted to achieve. So, I sat and thought about it.

As I concentrated, a little voice spoke to me.

'You can't write a book. What makes you think you can be an author?'

This belief was going to be a barrier to my success, because if I kept saying it to myself and believing it why would I even start? So I asked myself, 'Is that what I want?' The answer was clearly, 'No!' So then I asked myself, 'So, Andrew, what do you want?' This is what I came up with:

'I write brilliantly. I am a bestselling published author. My book is making a difference in the lives of others.'

When I said that positive statement to myself a couple of times, I immediately felt better. I was empowered and I noticed the anxiety slightly lessen. Okay, what else may be holding me back? I concentrated again and again this voice spoke to me:

'You don't have a nutritional qualification, so no-one will want to read your book.'

This was a big one to overcome — this limiting-belief would again stop me from even trying. So I again asked myself, 'Is that what I want?' The answer was again 'No!' So then I asked myself, 'So, Andrew, what do you want?' This is what I came up with:

'I have great practical knowledge about the power of nutrition and I communicate it in a way that empowers people to take positive action. I am totally qualified to write an amazing nutritional-based book.'

Again saying this statement to myself made me feel strong and confident almost immediately. I was getting more and more excited. What next? I thought again and the voice came to me:

'You don't have the time or energy to fit anything else into your already crazy schedule.'

It was obvious this one would rear its ugly head at some stage. Unless I could believe there was a way to find time in my 100-plus hour work week I would be finished before I even began. So again I asked myself, 'Is that what I want?' The answer again was absolutely, 'No!' So I asked myself, 'So, Andrew, what do you want?' This is what I came up with:

'I easily prioritise and find the time to write my book and the excitement of getting it finished provides me with unlimited energy all day long.'

I spent the next 30 minutes or so delving in and digging out all of the lingering and nagging doubts that were causing my anxiety — it was a long list. The good news is I was able to turn that long list of limiting beliefs into a long list of positive and empowering statements. So at the end of this challenging process I felt great, as I could see real hope, and I started to feel absolute belief I could write this book.

I started a daily regime of reading these new empowering statements out aloud as I looked at myself in the mirror. Simple yes, easy no! It was incredibly confronting because I was dealing with years and years of firmly established beliefs and, at times, I didn't believe what I was telling myself, but I kept going. I kept thinking about how I would feel and how my life would be once this book was finished and that allowed me to move through the discomfort.

Each morning I rose, looked at myself in the mirror and thought ... *'You sexy beast!'* Then I wiped the sleep out of my eyes, looked again and thought ... *'Aaagh, who are you?'* I came to terms with how I looked, I repeated those positive statements and each day I believed a little bit more and grew more confident in my ability. Eventually I knew deep in my heart and believed totally I was going to be a published author.

Secret author's business ... the steps to success:

In the previous chapter I discussed having a dream and a burning desire to lead you to a firm decision to be a published author. Without this decision nothing will start and without belief nothing will continue. The good news is, if you have done the activities from the previous chapter, then you are committed to the journey. The question now is, do you totally believe that you will be successful?

You may, like me, be able to logically look at the process and intellectually agree it can be done. The challenge is that rarely do we do things that are logical! Do you know what I mean? The voice in your head will tell you what you believe about yourself. What is it saying? Is it saying, 'I can, I will, I am good enough'? Or is it saying, 'I'm not sure, I have doubts, I don't know if I am good enough?' Whatever you are saying will eventuate in your life — whether you like it or not!

When you think about holding your amazing published book in your hands what and how do you feel? If you are anything like me there will be conflicting feelings — excitement and anxiety! The excitement is the result of positive feelings associated with your achievement. These we need to feed. The anxiety is created by self-doubt and negative beliefs. These we need to replace.

No matter how much you want the result, no matter how strong the desire and no matter how hard you work you will only ever achieve what you, deep down, believe you will achieve. So, are you ready to get rid of the negative and destructive beliefs and replace them with positive and empowering ones?

Say yes!

Key questions and actions steps:

1. When you think about holding your own published book in your hands, do you feel any anxiety? Think very carefully here, because it may not be obvious.

2. On a separate sheet of paper write a list of the causes of that anxiety. In other words what are the challenges and obstacles you feel will be a barrier to writing your book? Get them all out of your head and onto paper.

3. Look at each one of those limiting beliefs and ask yourself, 'Is that what I want?'

4. On another sheet of paper write *exactly what you want* for each one. This will result in a list of powerful, positive and present tense affirmations.

5. Now, the fun bit. Take that first sheet of paper, the one with all the negative, yucky limiting beliefs on it and tear it into little pieces. As you destroy it say, 'Goodbye you will never hold me back again, you are gone from my life forever.' Then throw it away, flush it down the toilet or burn it! As it leaves, feel yourself getting lighter. Feel the heaviness of those negative thoughts disappear forever.

6. Now, could you commit to reading these new positive affirmations to yourself, looking in the mirror, every day, even if you don't feel like it? This is the key to your success!

7. What and who are you currently listening to, reading and watching that may be holding you back and feeding your lack of self-belief?

8. Who are the most positive and encouraging people in your life? Could you choose to spend more time with them?

9. Would you be willing to read positive uplifting books such as the *Magic of Thinking Big* by David Schwarz, *The Slight Edge* by Jeff Olsen or *Dance Until It Rains* by Andrew Jobling?

10. Would you be willing watch less TV, spend less time on the internet and spend more time listening to positive and empowering programs and audios?

Chapter Nine

How did that happen?

*"Two years after I had unreasonably and illogically decided
to become a published author, with really no qualifications,
no writing skills and no idea what I was doing it actually happened!
Proud, excited and, to be honest, a bit stunned I held in
my hands my first two published books."*

As I sat down to start writing my mind was racing with questions: *'Where do I start? How do I structure this? How many chapters? How long should the chapters be? How do I transition between chapters?'* These were just a few of the questions running through my head. I realised at that moment a harsh truth — I really had no idea what I was doing! I needed a plan of some sort.

The cogs and gears in my head started turning, my eyes started spinning and smoke started shooting out of my ears but then somehow and from somewhere, deep in the recesses of my brain, I discovered a starting point. That starting point was ...the end! Yep, my brain works in weird and wonderful ways! But, it made sense to me. If I know what the end looks like then I can work out a plan to get there. Just like when I am heading somewhere in my car;

if I know where I am going then I can work out the best way to get there.

I thought very carefully about the message I wanted to portray. I thought about what I wanted the readers to know when they finished the book. I thought about how I wanted readers to feel in response to reading the book. I thought about what I wanted them to do as a result of reading the book. After some time and purposeful reflection I was clear about where I was headed and what I wanted the impact of the book to have on the readers.

I wanted it to be engaging and informative enough so that the reader would be compelled to read all the way to the end. I wanted them to understand how simple being lean, fit and healthy through good nutrition really is. I wanted that same person to then feel relieved and excited and to say, 'I can do that ... I will do that!' I wanted them to be empowered to take immediate action and clear about exactly what they needed to do. Most importantly, I wanted them to say, 'This book has changed my life and I look and feel amazing!'

The rest was actually quite easy. I imagined the person reading the book was coming from a point of ignorance and I had to lead them to a point of knowledge and positive, empowered action. Simple!

I listed the steps in this process of taking someone from knowing nothing to achieving the desired result. I ended up with around 15–20 bullet points and this became a very rough chapter outline. Wow, that was simple! The only other thing I had to think about was how long the chapters would be and how I should write this book.

Well this was simple because I thought about me, 'the

super-reader'. Not! What would keep me engaged in reading? I thought if I could write a book that I would read then, based on my propensity for reading, it would be a book that almost anyone could read — even a five-year-old!

Every time I start reading a book, even now, I flick through and see how long the chapters are. If they are short I am much more motivated to start reading because I know I can finish at least one chapter — an awesome achievement for me! If the chapters are too long then I am less inclined to even start that book and I may even look for another book with shorter chapters. So, I concluded I needed to keep the chapters short.

My disinclination for reading came from being forced to read school books full of dry information and facts and if I lasted five minutes that was a good effort. So whilst this was a non-fiction book it had to be engaging. Books that kept me engaged were stories, had case studies and incorporated some humour. Okay, that is how I needed to write my book. There was now only one more decision to make.

As I thought about my academic history with my lack of commitment to study, reading, writing and generally anything to do with the English subject, I wondered whether I should do some sort of writing course. Should I learn how to structure sentences and paragraphs? Should I learn how to write more eloquently? I wondered whether I should learn anything due to my undeniable lack of any appropriate skills.

To be honest, I didn't think about it for too long! Firstly I didn't have the time to go and do more learning. Secondly, it would slow down my progress. Thirdly, and most importantly, it just wasn't me! I have my own uniqueness and my own style that, I believed, would make my book different and even better than any other book on the market. I don't need someone to teach me how to write, to change my style or to smother my individual uniqueness. This book was already in me. I just need to believe in myself and let it out. So, that's what I did and that's what I teach every other aspiring author to do — tap into the amazing author that is already inside and just let him or her out!

Would it be perfect? Hmmm, let me think about that for a micro-second ...absolutely not! But, isn't that what an editor and proofreader is for? All I had to do was write the book to the best of my limited ability and then let a trained professional fix it for me (or at least tell me what I needed to do to get it to a publishable state). That was enough analysing and rationalising for me. I was ready to get started!

I was excited, I was focused, I was confident and I was a bit crazy! Even so, the thought of this daunting task scared me. I estimated about 50,000 words ... yikes! How was I going to do that? I stressed over it for a short time and then I just broke it down into small chunks. The thought of writing 50,000 words was totally terrifying and intimidating, but writing 500 words wasn't. I thought about how long it would take me to write 500 words, and I came up with 15–30 minutes. That I could do!

If I simply wrote 500 words each day, it would take just 100 days to have a 50,000-word manuscript! An investment of a mere 15–30 minutes each day, and in just over three months I would have a manuscript ready to go to the next phase. I was immediately excited and empowered again. I started and I didn't stop until it was done.

I was able to find pockets of time. It wasn't 15–30 minutes every day. Sometimes it was an hour here, 20 minutes there and over four months guess what? With that burning desire and following the principle of one word and one day at a time I had written a 50,000-word manuscript! I couldn't quite believe it, but boy was I proud!

Okay, now what?

Simple, find a publisher who loves my manuscript! I have to admit here that I don't have the inspiring story of the author who had to overcome dozens and dozens of rejected submissions from publishers. I can't say I was living in the streets and eating scraps out of garbage cans with my unpublished manuscript as my only hope for survival. I wish I could tell you the story which includes the great pain, suffering and my overcoming insurmountable odds to get my book published, but instead I hate to say that my first two books were actually quite easily published!

My uncle and his son own a publishing house in Melbourne, Australia. Hey, we all know people, don't we? We all have relatives that help us out. Some people have mechanics in their family and get cheap repairs. Some have hairdressers and get cheap hair treatments. Others are related to accountants and get their tax done for free. It just happened that I was related to publishers — my good fortune! I will be forever grateful to my uncle and cousin for helping me through what can be a challenging and character-building process.

Getting my manuscript looked at by them was obviously easy. Having them actually accept the manuscript, even though they were family, was not quite as easy because it still had to be a commercially-viable proposition. So when they said they would publish it I knew it had to be good enough for them to think it would be profitable. They even asked me to write another book for them, one to go into a series of wellness books they produced. Of course I said yes!

So two years after I had unreasonably and illogically decided to become a published author, with really no qualifications, no writing skills and no idea what I was doing it actually happened! Proud, excited and to be honest a bit stunned I held, in my hands, my first two published books: *Eat Chocolate, Drink Alcohol and be Lean and Healthy* (*Eat Choc* for short) and *Simply Strength*. Both, by the way, became best-sellers!

There is no doubt about it I am an accidental best-selling author!

Secret author's business ... the steps to success:

Am I special? To my mum, dad and wife I am, but no, I'm not any more special than you! Did I do anything mind-blowing to be a published author? No! Did I do anything that required massive effort, sacrifice or pain? Not in the least! Did I do anything that other people can't do? No way, anyone can do it! You can do it!

So, what did I do? First, I made a decision that my book would be written no matter what! Second, I focused on doing exactly that; doing the things that would bring me success. Third, and probably most importantly, I got into action and I did something positive every single day whether I felt like it or not!

Let's face it, it doesn't matter how fired-up you are, how

much you believe in yourself, how educated you may be or how talented you are, without daily action nothing will happen!

You may have heard the saying that goes something like, 'the dog in the fight doesn't notice the fleas'. In other words, the dog is so focused on success and survival that it has no time to worry about an insignificant flea. When you are in action, with a positive focus, you don't seem to worry about the small stuff. The other great saying is, 'action cures fear'. The most amazing thing about positive motion is that it immediately, totally and magically removes your doubts and fears!

I simply committed to writing a small amount every single day — no matter if I was motivated to write or not. If you wait until you are motivated you will go nowhere. Don't rely on motivation, rely on good habits. I knew if I wrote every day, whether I was motivated or not, excited or not, energised or fatigued, no matter how I felt, eventually I would create a habit that would lead to success.

Make no mistake about it, making an excuse not to write on any given day will also become a habit — unfortunately a habit that leads to disappointment and regret. The question is what result do you want? Which habit will you commit to?

Consider this simple formula: writing 500 words takes 15–30 minutes. If you simply write 500 words per day for 100 days you have written a 50,000-word manuscript! That is just over three months to finish a manuscript and have it ready to start the publishing process. You can do that!

I will discuss steps to publishing in the following chapters.

Key questions and actions steps:

1. Have you made a decision to do whatever it takes to have a written and published book?

2. What is an achievable deadline for you to complete the first draft of your manuscript?

3. Are you willing to commit time to your book every day? That is every day, no matter how small the amount of time. Creating the habit is what we are working on here.

4. Assuming you answered 'yes' to the above three questions, here are some steps to consider:
    a. Get excited and do something every day!
    b. Read your goals, visions and affirmations every day. Imagine the feeling of success!
    c. Develop a rough chapter outline, listing the steps (chapters) to take someone from 'ignorance' to 'competence'. In other words, what are the steps you need to lead the reader from knowing nothing about your book to what you want them to know, the way you want them to feel and behave by the time they have finished it?
    d. The clearer you are about the impact you want your book to have on the reader the easier it will be to plan and to write.
    e. Make the decision that you will write every day — then the rest is easy!
    f. How many words will you commit to as a daily minimum?

g. What are the things you can put on hold whilst you are writing your manuscript (TV, social activities, social media etc)?

h. Find a mentor or someone who will help, encourage and guide you when you are challenged. I am here, ready and willing to help you (andrew@ andrewjobling.com.au).

i. Do it even when you don't feel like it.

j. Trust yourself. You are good enough to write this book. It is inside of you — just let it flow out!

k. Use stories, anecdotes and case studies to engage the reader whether you are writing fiction or non-fiction.

l. Keep the chapters short 1000–3000 words. People like me need to have achievable targets when they start reading a book/chapter.

m. There is no need to keep editing or to ask other people their opinion as you go ... you may never finish! Just write it all and fix what needs fixing when you have finished.

n. Have fun — enjoy the process and stay focused on the result.

Trouble shooting potential challenges:

Symptom:

- You are having trouble staying focused, prone to making excuses, getting distracted easily and procrastinating.

Cause(s):

1. You have not yet emotionally connected writing your book with what is most important to you.

2. Your negative self-talk is winning.

Solution(s):

1. Go back and re-read the work you did in Chapter 7 — connect deeply with the things that are most important to you and the reasons why writing your book will help to achieve them.
2. Re-focus on your affirmations. Read them twice per day if necessary. Increase your exposure to positive people, books and audios.

Eat Chocolate, Drink Alcohol and be Lean & Healthy

Simply Strength

Chapter Ten

The passion begins

"Who knew I could possibly have such a profound impact on the lives of other people? People I didn't even know! It was incredibly mind-blowing, but also unbelievably empowering. I was hooked — the start of my new obsession!"

All by accident I had discovered the most burning passion I had or have ever found (with the exception of my beautiful wife Laura). Initially I thought it was sport but I now realise that was just a phase in my life to teach me some tough but valuable lessons and to increase my confidence.

Then I thought it was personal training. Wrong again! A wise person once said, "Choose a job you love, and you will never have to work a day in your life." I hate to say it, but this time they've got it wrong! I loved and was incredibly passionate about personal training, but after 15 years of getting up at 5am and working till 9pm that love and passion were stripped back to become a painful and all-consuming chore!

Writing was it for me — who could have possibly predicted? Certainly not I! I really had no idea if my books would sell. I had no idea if anyone would read them and, if they did, I had no idea what they would say. Then not long after the release of *Eat Choc* this newly discovered passion was cast in iron when I received this email from someone I had never met:

> *Andrew, I googled your name wondering if you have written another book and discovered your email address. Your book has had a profound effect on my life. My 14-year-old son bought the book for me for Christmas as he was concerned about my weight. Ironically he bought it from the Margaret River Chocolate Factory while we were on holiday. It has changed my life. I stopped weighing myself after I had lost 25 kgs from 110kgs and use my belt and watch band to gauge my progress. My whole family has embraced GI and your holistic approach towards life-exercise, nutrition, etc. I push your book to everyone who asks how I did it. Thank you.*

No long after that I received this:

> *Dear Andrew, I just wanted to write you a little note to say thank you for the wonderful information that you provided in your book, 'Eat Chocolate, Drink Alcohol and be Lean and Healthy'. Words cannot describe how thankful I am to have picked up your book ... for the first time in my life things began to make sense. I have previously done a lot of reading about dieting, food and general well-being ... but no other publication hit home as much as yours did. The whole concept of being caught on the 'blood-sugar rollercoaster' was instantly chilling ... I knew instantly that this rollercoaster was controlling my life. Despite eating 'healthily' I would often skip breakfast and binge on sugar in the afternoon ... oh, how things have changed now. I am so grateful that I found your book when I did. I am currently 21 and in many ways was on a dangerous path ... not necessarily with food and exercise but*

mainly with my self-esteem and feeling like a failure. I have never had any issues with weight however in the last two years found myself getting a little heavier month by month. I have applied your advice and strategies almost with ease ... it is a far easier and rewarding program than some of the destructive diets that I have tried ... I cringe when I think about what I put my body through. Andrew, thank you so much for your words ... I will never forget the experience of reading your book. You have helped me in so many ways — I cannot thank you enough.

Who knew I could possibly have such a profound impact on the lives of other people? People I didn't even know! It was incredibly mind-blowing, but also unbelievably empowering. I was doing what I had always wanted to do — making a difference in the lives of people I didn't even know. I was hooked. Writing was the start of my new obsession!

As a result of being a published author I was getting more speaking engagements at different places. I was getting gigs on radio and writing spots for magazines and newspapers. All of a sudden I was in demand! I had magically transformed into an expert and a leader in my field. How? Simply because I had decided to take my knowledge and experience and do what everyone can do, many people want to do, but only a few will. I was no different than before, I was no more knowledgeable than before and my message hadn't changed. In fact, nothing about me had changed — except that I was now a published author.

I'd really found my place in life. I was doing what I had always done, that is, helping people to be fitter, leaner, happier and healthier, but now I could impact more people rather than just working one-on-one with them. I had a new lease on life and a refreshed vision!

I had always had a love for public speaking, which I guess was that need to be centre of attention. For many years before the books I had been trying to establish myself as a professional speaker, but was continually hitting road-blocks. I remembered that one meeting I had with a speaker agency as I was trying to get them to represent and promote me as a corporate speaker. They asked me if I had written a book. I told them I was in the process of writing it. They then said to me there was no point continuing the conversation and to come back when I had a published book!

It was amazing the doors and opportunities that opened up once those first two books were published. It gave me instantaneous credibility as, all of a sudden, I was now an expert. Why? Because I had written a book so I must be! Life was suddenly exciting and incredibly busy.

I now had only one obstacle — time! I was working 12–15 hour days in a business that I couldn't remove myself from. Whilst I was there I couldn't do the writing and speaking I wanted to do. So after 15 years of personal training I knew I needed to find a way out. The question was how do I create time, without losing my income so I can focus on this new and incredibly burning passion of mine?

I was determined not to make the same mistake I had with my personal training career. I had relied on it for my income and it was my sole income stream. When I started as a personal trainer I would bounce out of bed at 5am excited about another day of helping change lives. After 15 years in this career and relying on it for my income I don't think bouncing out of bed is how I would describe it. Getting shoved out of bed was more like it!

I made a decision regarding my new passion of writing — that it would *always* be my true passion. I didn't want to make the same mistake I'd made with personal training and rely on it for my income. To ensure that would be the case I had to somehow remove any dependence on needing to make money from it. I decided I needed to separate my income into two areas: money to live off and money I would create through my writing, speaking and associated passionate pursuits. My only challenge, at that time, was how to do it!

I'm not sure if you believe in the law of attraction and I don't know if, at that time, I did either. Nevertheless, just as I was looking for answers a friend of mine handed me a book called *Rich Dad, Poor Dad* by Robert Kiyosaki. This particular book slapped me around and made me realise where I had been going wrong for so long.

Until that point in my life I had been working for more than 15 years. The mistake I had been making was that I'd been spending my time instead of investing it. I had been spending time trading my hours for an active income. In other words if I didn't work, I didn't earn. No wonder I was so exhausted!

Kiyosaki helped me to understand that the only way to enjoy time *and* money was to invest some of my hours building income-producing assets. His book didn't explain how this could be done, it did, however, make me fully aware that I was totally misguided in my current approach. I was just grateful I wasn't 20 years older before I found out this news. Up until that point I was only doing what I knew, which is what I'd been taught for many years. It was time to start to do some un-learning and re-learning.

It was a book that made me aware of what I didn't know, so maybe, I thought, books can teach me what I need to know to get the financial result I want. I started on an intensive journey of personal development: reading, listening to success audios, attending seminars and working with people who had the result I wanted. I changed my thinking, I changed my associations and I changed my habits. Guess what? I changed my situation!

One of the books I read talked about the idea of giving up what you want in the short-term to get it back in abundance for the long-term ... so, I did. For the next 12 months I wrote less and invested extra spare time outside of my busy life to creating a passive income. This enabled me to go from working 80–90 hours per week to 30-40 hours a week without losing any income!

It really worked. For just 12 months I invested five–ten hours per week that I would rather have spent writing to be rewarded with 50 hours per week that I could use any way I wanted! It was amazing and a dream come true because now I could focus on my passions which were writing, speaking and helping others. The best news was that I could now do it for the love and passion, and not because I needed the money. The money however was, and is, very nice!

Secret author's business ... the steps to success:

We all were asked the wrong question when we were young! We were asked, 'What do you want to do when you grow up?' That question leads many people down a path they later regret. As a child, the idea of being a policeman, doctor, lawyer or other similar profession sounds exciting and glamorous (as personal trainer did for me). Let's be brutally honest here — there is nothing glamorous about working long, hard hours and sacrificing your health, your time with people you love and the time to do the things you are passionate about.

The question we should've been asked as children, and the question we should be asking our children now is, 'How do you want to live?' Had I been asked that question, like most people I suspect, I would have answered, 'I want great health, lots of money and lots of time to do the things I am passionate about, with the people I love'. Most professions will not lead to this outcome but, in fact, lead in the opposite direction!

As you consider writing your book and creating a new career path, it's important you have a clear picture of exactly how you want to be living your life. Then, make sure the career you engineer for yourself will actually lead you to this reality.

Key questions and actions steps:

1. Describe in writing the exact scenario you would like to be living: the income you make, your career, the energy you have, how you are able to spend your time, what you are able to do and who are you are able to help, etc.

2. Is what you are currently doing leading you to achieve this in the next five years?

3. Are you prepared to make some changes to achieve this lifestyle?

4. If you haven't already, in addition to your book(s), start to research some viable options that will start to produce a passive income over the next two to five years.

5. Once you are a published author, what other opportunities can you see this creating for yourself?

6. Make a list of the things you will do to ensure that you are successful.

You will start to understand more about how to implement these ideas as you continue to read this book.

*In store …
how exciting!*

In advertisement … very exciting!

Dimmie sinner's saved by a Saint

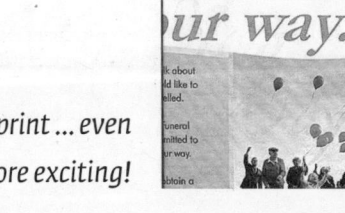

*In print … even
more exciting!*

The expert.

On the cover!

The speaker.

The radio shows.

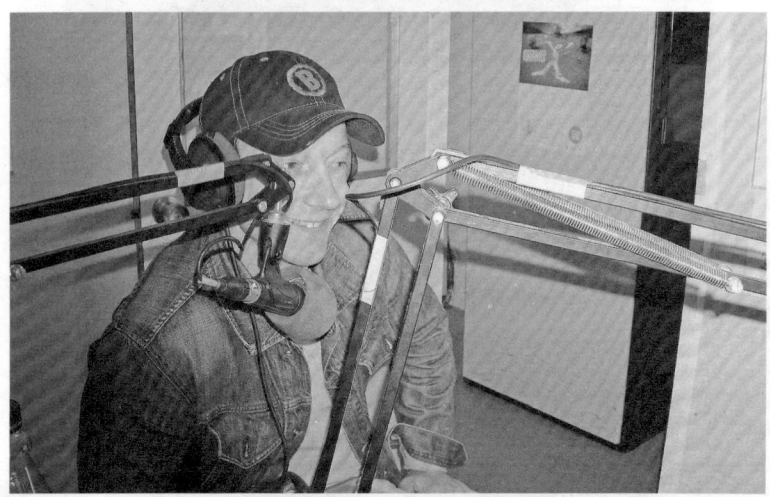

Chapter Eleven

A new mission!

"For hours we talked, we laughed, we cried. I listened and I wrote. At the end I was even more proud and inspired by Mum than before, and totally determined this book would be written."

Through much of my adult life — as I was struggling to find myself, my passion and my direction — I had an inspiring person beside me and behind me, encouraging me to keep going when I felt like giving up. It was my mum, Sue.

Although she hated me playing because she was worried I would hurt myself, she was my number one fan during my football career. Even as a child she was such a powerful and positive influence in my life. I have a particularly fond memory from when I was eight years old (over 40 years ago as I write this) that seems like it was yesterday ...

I had won the award for 'Best and Fairest' at the junior football club for which I played. At the end-of-season barbecue the awards were presented and the last trophy for the day was the prestigious 'Best and Fairest'. My name was called and excitedly I ran up to collect it. I was asked to make a short speech and all of a sudden my mind went blank! What could I say? I didn't want to make a fool of myself. Then, after a few uncomfortable moments, it just came to me — the one thing that, throughout that whole season, had impacted me the most. I stood up tall with pride and I said with love, 'I would just like to thank my mum for driving me to training!'

She was there watching at my first senior level game with St Kilda when I got knocked out and carried off on a stretcher. She was there for me when I was a cheeky teenager and often in trouble with teachers, neighbours and even the law! She was always there for me through the ups and downs of my relationships and the many other challenges in my life — she was, is and will always be my hero.

When I was in my mid-twenties and in my teaching years she was diagnosed with breast cancer. I can remember the day clearly. It was June 1988. This particular day was a Friday and I was just about to go into the class I liked to teach the least — Year 10 Mathematics. It was a double lesson after lunch and the last session before the weekend, so you can imagine how interested 15-year-olds were in learning about trigonometry and algebra.

Ten minutes before the end of lunch, just as I was about to head to class, I received a call from my dad. I couldn't remember the last time he'd called me, so I knew this had to be something serious. He's always very matter of fact and this call was no exception. He simply explained to me that Mum had just been diagnosed with breast cancer.

Wow, this was the last thing I had expected! There were a few moments of total disbelief. It felt almost like it was a dream — a bad dream. I was stunned and speechless as I stood there holding the phone by my side until my dad's voice broke the silence, 'Andrew, are you okay?' I couldn't tell if I was okay or not as I was numb! My eyes welled with tears, my heart sank and I felt totally helpless. Then the reality of where I was hit me; I had a class to teach. I am not sure how I held it together, but I taught that class. What I taught, I can't quite remember! I didn't care at that point, I just wanted to get out of there and get to my mum as fast as I could.

The whole family was in shock. How could this happen? Why us? Why my mother? She was only in her fifties and with so much life still left to live. It scared me. I wanted it to just go away and so I didn't want to know too much. I stuck my head in the sand and pretended everything was okay. Not a bad short-term strategy, but at some stage this attitude was destined to bite me in the butt ...the one sticking out of the sand!

After initial treatment and associated side effects, she was given the 'all clear' by the doctors that the cancer was gone and there was a very good chance it would never return. We all breathed a sigh of relief and in no time all of us, including Mum, had slipped back into our lives as they had been before the diagnosis. Again, not a good long-term strategy!

We had all mistakenly believed luck had a part to play in this initial diagnosis and prognosis. We thought it was bad luck that she was diagnosed in the first place and great luck that she was cured. We didn't, for a second, consider that it was a sign that things needed to change in our lives, particularly that of my mother. We didn't stop to reflect on Mum's actions and habits. We didn't consider that maybe her poor habits led to this unfortunate consequence.

Well, things changed quickly when, some 18 months later, the cancer reappeared in her liver. The initial optimistic opinion of the doctor regarding her first episode changed as this new condition was diagnosed. Their next prognosis was not at all optimistic as they gave her only a few more years to live but they didn't know my mum! Her attitude was that they were wrong the first time, so what makes them right this time!

So she took the conventional medical opinions with a grain of salt attitude. She didn't believe what those doctors had predicted for her — after all she had a life to live, things to do, places to go and people to love. As a result, she took matters into her own hands and the next 15 years were filled with persistence, strength, love, joy and happiness. They were years where she taught me the power of a decision and the strength of an attitude independent of even the most challenging circumstances. My mum is my hero and she inspired me then, as her memory continues to inspire me today.

It was in September 2004, more than 16 years after the initial diagnosis. I was on a holiday on the Gold Coast with my mum and dad and my partner, at that time. At this point my mum had been battling her breast and liver cancer for 16 years and during those years, as I mentioned, she had absolutely inspired me with her vision, her courage, her determination and her incredible attitude and will to live a great life no matter the circumstances. It was then I got the idea for my next and best book. I made a decision during that week away that I was going to write a book about my mum; share her story and the lessons to inspire the world.

We had a great week as a family and I particularly wanted to spend some special time with Mum to talk to her about her life and journey with the disease. So, on one of the days

I told her that I was planning to write a book about her life to highlight some valuable lessons that could benefit others. Her response was, 'Why would anyone be interested in my story?' She had such humility and quiet determination about her which I struggle to find the words to describe.

Nevertheless, she started telling me her story. From her beginning as a young child born in Hungary just before the Second World War, her journey to Australia, her insecurities as she grew up, her romance with my dad and her joys and challenges as a mother. Finally to her diagnosis with cancer and the life-altering journey for the next 16 years. For hours we talked, we laughed, we cried. I listened and I wrote. At the end I was even more proud and inspired by Mum than before, and totally determined this book would be written.

Secret author's business ... the steps to success:

Passion is the key! No matter what you are doing, you need to do it with passion, powerful emotion and love in your heart. You will know, from the books you have read, those words that have been written with true passion are the ones that engage, inspire and impact the reader most. Would you agree?

Find the passion for your writing and you will write a wonderfully inspiring book — whether fiction or non-fiction. The thought of my mother: her nature, her life, the things she did and the person she was still warms my heart and brings tears to my eyes. The question for you is what brings tears to your eyes? I can't remember the amount of tears I shed as I was writing *Dance Until It Rains* but I must have gone through several keyboards! The end result was so worth it.

Find your passion and your book will be a winner.

Key questions and actions steps:

1. What makes you cry?

2. What is it about your book you are passionate about?

3. How can you become more passionate and emotionally connected to your book?

4. How will your book inspire others?

5. How will your book impact lives?

6. How will your book change your own life?

7. What is the main message of the book?

8. How is that personal and powerfully emotional for you?

One eyed!

My beautiful mother.

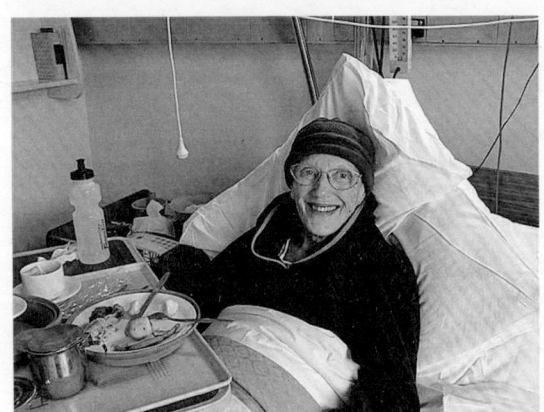

My hero.

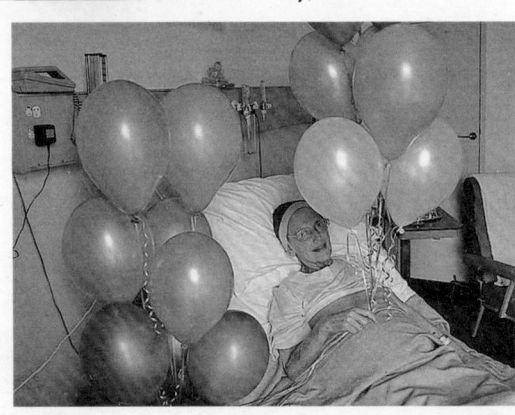

*An inspiration to
the very end.*

Chapter Twelve

Learning to dance until it rains!

"This was obviously poetic justice because of the ease at which I got my first two books published! The universe had just sent me a message loud and clear ... THIS ONE YOU ARE GOING TO HAVE TO WORK FOR!"

Well, I fully intended to write the book, but often we have great plans and then along comes life to bite us in the butt! What my mum and dad hadn't told me, or my brother and sister, was that her condition wasn't improving. In fact, the doctors were fast running out of options. My parents were always protecting us from the reality which was her day-to-day battle for life.

It was only a couple of months after this trip to Queensland that, due to an extreme course of radiotherapy, my mum's condition rapidly deteriorated. She went from being an active, mobile and vibrant woman to being so incapacitated that even sitting up in bed was a huge challenge.

The one thing, however, that didn't change was her 'never give in' attitude and the beautiful smile with freshly applied lipstick that was always on her face! That is the last memory I have of my mum as she slipped into her final peaceful state on December 3, 2004.

I had 16 years to deal with the fact that my mum had cancer and that there was a chance that she may die before her time — but did I? Not for one second! My head was buried far too deeply in the sand just hoping it would all go away. So when the inevitable happened I was devastated. The next 12 months were an absolute write off. The only thing that happened, within that period of time, to distract my mourning for my mum was the breakdown of my long-term relationship. When it rains ...

Over the next couple of years my life was really all about trying to make some sense of the things that had happened and why. It was a confusing time and so any thought of a book was at the farthest reaches of my mind. But, as they say, 'time heals all', as does perspective and a desire to find the good in all situations. I started to write spasmodically over the next couple of years and got about halfway into the manuscript. The decision finally came in May 2008, whilst I was on my honeymoon with my beautiful wife Laura, that it was time to finish what I'd started. With that, I got back to work — this time with a determined focus to finish the manuscript.

Once it was finally finished I was excited. I thought it would be a simple job to send it to my publishers and then let them do the rest. Rather confidently I drafted the email, attached the manuscript and sent it to the publishers. I then waited in excited anticipation for their positive response. For the next 48 hours I sat in front of my computer, hitting 'send/receive' every few minutes until ... it finally arrived!

The email I was waiting for with such excitement and

anticipation didn't have the answer I was expecting or hoping for. I read it once then I rubbed my eyes and I read it again. I pinched myself to make sure I was awake, and again I read it to make sure I was actually seeing what was written on that computer screen ... the publishers *were not* going to take on and publish this amazing book! It took a while for this baffling outcome to register. My relatives who own a publishing company were not going to publish the book about my mum! What would I do now?

Whilst I was in unchartered waters in terms of publishing a book, I'd been here before many times during my life. As disappointed as I was, I had an inner feeling and confidence that it would work out. So, after the initial shock and some purposeful reflection, the answer became quite clear to me ... get on the phone and start making calls!

That's exactly what I did. I hit Google hard and got a list of every major publisher in Australia. I started making calls, following each publisher's submission guidelines and I started sending out my manuscript. I sent out about 25 manuscripts and then ... I waited patiently.

I waited and I waited and I kept on waiting. Then finally, after many weeks, I received a package in the mail. I was excited. I was sure it would be good news! It was, however, my manuscript with a very polite but very definite rejection letter included. Oh well, there are many more to go. Soon after I received another. Just as excited I opened it to find another rejection letter. Then I got another, and another, and another! Out of the 25 manuscripts I sent, I received about 5 rejection letters. I'm still waiting to hear back from the other 20 publishing houses ... since 2008!

This was obviously poetic justice because of the ease at

which I got my first two books published! The universe had just sent me a message loud and clear ... THIS ONE YOU ARE GOING TO HAVE TO WORK FOR!

I was up for the challenge. I had faith. I knew there was a publisher out there who would take it on because it was a great book and I believed it would make a difference in people's lives. So I kept patiently waiting and hoping that the next letter I received would be the one I was hoping for. That letter never came!

After many months of rejection I started to doubt myself and my manuscript and wondered whether this was ever going to happen. But then I thought about my mum; her attitude, her resilience, her determination. I thought about the title of the book, *Dance Until It Rains* and the story which inspired it:

The story is about the Red Indians living off the land in the prairies and plains of the United States of America. This was a very challenging time. The land had suffered from drought for a long period and the tribes were suffering as a result of the lack of water, lack of vegetation and lack of food.

But, across the land, and in this time of desperation, the legend grew of the tribe that would dance and make it rain.

The other tribes assumed they could do the same and so set the goal to make it rain. Some would dance for 20–30 minutes but stop with no success. Others would dance for hours until their feet blistered and give up. Some tribes would even dance for days on end but give in to their aching backs and the ridicule from neighbouring tribes. They would all give up disheartened and just as dry as when they started.

A decision was finally made to track down this legendary tribe and find the secret to their success. So the chiefs from all the tribes took off in search of this one tribe. When they found the tribe, they sat at the feet of its chief and pleaded; "Oh great chief, we have tried to make it rain, we are suffering, we need your help. How can you make it rain? What is your secret?"

"There is no secret," explained the chief, "Our method is simple — we dance until it rains."

Needless to say, I kept dancing!

Next approach — I started to contact literary agents the same way I did publishers. I got on Google again, made a list, started making calls and sending out manuscripts. It was a time consuming and costly exercise that resulted in the same outcome — rejection, after rejection, after rejection. I was discouraged, I was tired, I was emotional and I was over it! To be totally honest I was just about to give up, again, but this time I was serious.

Then, again, I thought about the book I had just written. I thought about my mum and her attitude. I thought about my iron-clad decision that it would be written. Ironically it was neither of those things that got me back onto the path. I thought about the message of the book I had just written — dance until it rains! Persist, overcome, keep going, never give-up. How could I possibly give-up? I had trapped myself into finishing the book.

Secret author's business ... the steps to success:

By following through, focusing on your passionate burning desire and writing a little every day you will eventually have a finished manuscript. This point, which should be the platform to the published book, is where many people get lost as they are not sure how to go about getting published. They may never even try because it just seems all too daunting, or they may make an initial attempt but give up because it seems too difficult.

If you 'dance until it rains' you will be a published author.

My first piece of advice is this — don't listen or take advice from anyone who hasn't successfully done what you are in the process of doing. People will tell you how hard it is to get published, how expensive it is to self-publish and what you should, shouldn't, can and can't do. They have no idea. Don't let someone else determine what you do or don't accomplish. Publishing is the fun bit. Finally all your hard work is leading to success and your dream is about to become reality. Get excited!

Your first decision is how you want to get your book published. Converting your book into and selling it as an e-book is a simple and effective process and one that you should definitely do. However, don't limit your publishing program to just an e-book. Having the hard-copy book is what you want. So then the decision is self-publishing or traditional publishing?

I have not self-published any of my books and I don't ever intend to. That doesn't mean you shouldn't, but before you decide to self-publish there are things to consider. It can certainly be a treacherous path and there are people out there who will give you bad advice and try to get your money. They will convince you that you won't get a traditional publisher and that you need to give them thousands of dollars to get it published.

They may teach you how to write a book, but you are already good enough to do that. They will produce a few hundred copies of your book which you have paid for but how good is the editing, proof-reading, design and quality? They will teach you how to market, distribute and sell your book but you will be on your own to do this. Most self-publishing companies, once they have your money and supplied your books, don't care whether you sell them or not.

I have seen far too often people invest time, money, blood, sweat and tears to write a book to then have hundreds, even thousands, of those books sit in boxes in their garage never sold or read because they didn't have the time, contacts, resources, desire or knowledge to get out and sell them. There are exceptions to this, but please be very careful about deciding to self-publish.

Traditional publishing, I believe, is the way to go and it isn't as hard as most people think it is. It certainly isn't as hard as I found it whilst trying to get *Dance Until It Rains* published. What I now know is that the secret lies in knowing where to find the right publishing house.

The right publishing house will:

- Assess your manuscript for free and advise you about its quality and what you need to do to get it to a commercially publishable state (if that is what you want).

- Communicate and partner with you through every step of the process.

- Invest in all or part of the publishing, PR, marketing, distributing and sales process.

- Agree with you on a contract and royalty/commission structure. They will have an ongoing financially-vested interest in the success of your book — that is good!

- Use professional editors, proof-readers, illustrators and designers to ensure the highest quality production.

- Appoint a PR person to get you media exposure and events to promote you and your book.

- Distribute the book into bookshops, libraries and international book fairs.

- Convert it to e-book format and put it on all the popular global platforms to sell it.

- Work with you to develop a career as an author and write multiple books — if that is what you want.

Doesn't that sound like a better idea?

I might sound biased — because I am. Whilst self-publishing may be a quicker way to get your book produced and may give you a bigger profit margin per book, the bottom line is you are 100 per cent responsible for the sales. I have always said I would rather 10 per cent of 1,000,000 sales than 100 per cent of 100 sales! If your book is good enough, why wouldn't it be published and why couldn't you sell 1,000,000 copies?

Key questions and actions steps:

1. Are you still trying to decide between self-publishing and traditional publishing?

2. Here are some questions to consider which will help with your decision. If you can answer 'yes' to all of the following questions then you would qualify as someone who could be successful through self-publishing:

   a. Do you have $5,000-$10,000 available to make sure you can produce a high quality, edited, proof-read, well-designed publication?

   b. Do you have, or are willing to invest in, the space to store many boxes of books?

   c. Do you have the time, inclination and energy to do your own marketing, PR, distribution and sales? That means set up a website, social media strategy, contact media, visit book shops, set up events, distribute and send books, etc? If the answer is 'no', do you have the resources to invest in someone to do this for you?

   d. Do you have a large social, business and personal network that would be an immediate captive market?

   e. Are you already speaking, running seminars, workshops and training that you could immediately sell your books at?

   f. Do you have a large database of people willing to refer you and your book to their own network and contacts?

3. If you have decided that self-publishing is not the best approach and are looking to find a traditional publishing house send me an email to andrew@ andrewjobling.com.au and I will send you details of where to send your manuscript so you can get the best possible publishing experience and path to achieving your dream.

Marrying my best friend.

My beautiful wife.

Our honeymoon.

Finishing the manuscript.

Chapter Thirteen

Getting back on the path to success!

"These are just a few of the things I did to keep myself going. Did I always do them all brilliantly? If I had, my book would have been finished much sooner than six-and-a-half years! But the main thing I knew was that it would be done, no matter how long it took."

After all the rejection, heartache, discouragement and disappointment it was such a tough job to keep myself on track to get *Dance Until It Rains* published. It was an emotional rollercoaster each and every day. Fired up and focussed one second and in a screaming heap on the floor the next. It really took a deliberate focus to not just stay on the path, but to get back on it every time I fell off.

It is interesting that there were times in that six-and-half years (the most challenging period of my life) when I didn't know whether I would survive. But not for one second did I entertain the thought that the book would not be written and published. It just wasn't an option! I was in the pits looking for that magic bullet to get me up and running again so many times. I remember during one pity-party episode when I forced myself to take a step back for a period of time. I started to think about why I was writing this book and I really thought about how it would impact my life.

I considered how my completed and published book would contribute positively to the eight areas of my life. I spent some time and divided my life into the following eight areas:

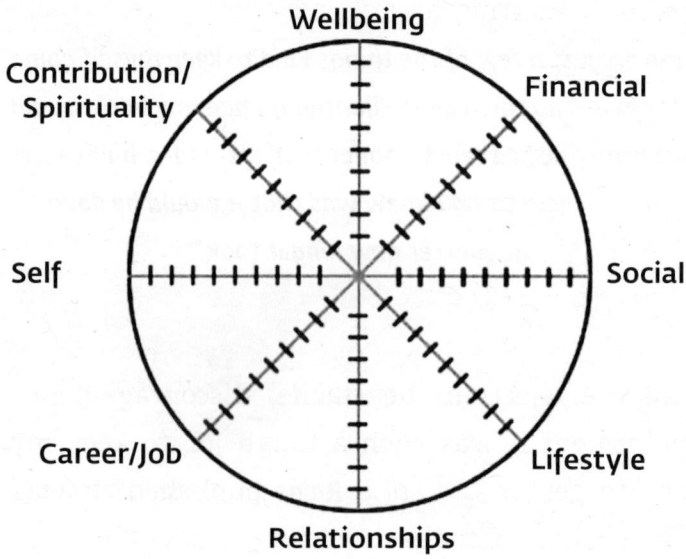

Then I thought about how this book would contribute to each area:

1. **Self:** It gives me confidence and self-esteem to know I can complete something that is, at times, challenging to say the least. I felt (and still feel) great about this book and the difference it's making in the lives of others.

2. **Relationships:** My marriage benefits from the lessons I learned from my mum. My relationship with

my dad, brother and sister gets stronger through this journey. My relationship with my (future) children will benefit from this lesson in love, devotion, courage and persistence.

3. **Wellbeing**: This definitely improves through taking more ownership of and responsibility for my own health through watching my mum and learning about her journey and the positive things she did.

4. **Career:** The book is enabling me to get more work; it increases my credibility and marketability as an in-demand speaker, writer and mentor.

5. **Financial:** The book increases my income through selling the book and the work that comes as a result of it.

6. **Social:** It is a great way for me to meet new people and relate better to people I already know.

7. **Lifestyle:** I work from home and love the lifestyle the book has contributed to.

8. **Spiritual/contribution:** This is a big one. My whole reason and philosophy is to help others and make a positive difference in their lives. I want to do this not so much by telling, but more through 'walking the talk'. This book totally contributes to this.

Having the book's completion powerfully connected to these eight areas of my life made the decision to keep going an easy one (despite all the challenges and obstacles). I am not saying the process was easy; I am saying the decision to stay in the race was easy. Once I had made this decision I always found a solution for any challenge that confronted me.

Speaking of always finding solutions, I love this story and I am sure you will too:

An old Italian man lived alone in New Jersey. He wanted to plant his annual tomato garden, but it was very difficult work as the ground was hard. His only son Vincent, who used to help him, was in prison. So the old man wrote a letter to his son and described his predicament:

"Dear Vinnie I am feeling very sad because it looks like I won't be able to plant my tomato garden this year. I am just getting too old to be digging up a garden plot. I know that if you were here my troubles would be over. I know that you would be happy to dig that plot for me like in the old days. Love Papa."

A few days later he received a letter from his son:

"Dear Papa, do not dig up the garden that is where all the bodies are buried. Love Vinnie."

At 3am the next morning FBI agents swarmed the place. Local police arrived with a warrant to search for bodies and they then dug up the entire area ...without finding any bodies. They apologised to the old man and left. That same day the old man received another letter from his son:

"Dear Papa, now go ahead and plant the tomatoes. That's the best I could do under the circumstances!"

Love it! Anything and everything is solvable!

I now knew I had to and would keep pushing towards my goal. I also knew I had to reduce and remove the negative forces holding me back, so in addition to focusing on what I wanted to achieve I really had to be prepared for any situation. This is what I did:

- I would always visualise when the book was published and how I would feel as a result. I did this every day, even when I didn't feel like it.

- I reduced my negative self-talk by focusing on and committing to a daily routine of affirmations and positive visualisation as I discussed in Chapter 8. I did this every day, even when I didn't feel like it.

- I read at least 15 minutes of a positive, uplifting book and listened to at least one positive audio CD every day. I did this every day, even when I didn't feel like it.

- I deliberately avoided negative people and chose to associate with people who would encourage me and my dream.

- I significantly reduced my TV watching and radio listening time to almost nothing, for two reasons. Firstly it created more time for me to do what I needed to do and, secondly, I was able to avoid all the bad news in the world and stay in my focused and positive space.

- Whenever I was confronted with a challenge, difficulty or problem, rather than complaining, blaming or feeling sorry for myself, I became good at asking myself, 'What is good about this?', 'What is the lesson?', and 'What is the solution to overcome it?' I thought about Vinnie and the tomatoes!

- I had a mentor who I could talk to when things got tough — someone who could give me the perspective and inspiration to keep going.

- I removed other distractions and simplified things in my life. I removed other activities that weren't adding to my life or contributing to my visions.

- I focused on my eating to ensure I would have optimal energy and be able to deal with stresses and emotional issues more effectively.

- I developed a routine of exercise, 20–30 minutes five days per week. It helped me feel strong and in control, it helped to clear my head and stay positive and it kept me feeling fit, healthy and energised!

- Every now and then I would have a tantrum and just 'spit the dummy' for a bit. Boy, it felt good! The important thing was that I didn't stay there for long; I got it out of my system, got over it and then kept going.

- I was fortunate to have the love and ongoing support of my beautiful wife, Laura, who was, and is always, there for me.

These are just a few of the things I did to keep myself going. Did I always do them all brilliantly? If I had, my book would have been finished much sooner than the six-and-a-half years it took! But the main thing I knew was that it would be done, because I would keep going no matter how long it took.

Secret author's business ... the steps to success:

I think this one is pretty self-explanatory. There's an interesting and slightly annoying principle in life — no matter what you are striving to achieve, you'll be tested to make sure you are serious about achieving it. Have you ever wondered why problems, distractions and challenges seem to arise just at the wrong time in life? Yep, it's a test! If you are serious about your goal you will learn from them, overcome them and become stronger as a result of them. If not, they will take you out!

No matter whether you are just getting started in the process of your book, well into the writing or maybe even at the publishing stage, get ready for life to test you. When it happens don't be surprised, disappointed or discouraged — be prepared. If you have done what I have suggested in the previous chapters you will see challenges, problems and adversity as stepping stones to greater things — like Vinnie did. If you haven't prepared yourself then, now is the time.

Key questions and actions steps:

1. Re-read your description of the life you are trying to create and how your book is a key part of achieving it. If you haven't done it yet — do it now. It will make a massive difference.

2. Read through my list above and create your own list of things you will do to stay positively and powerfully connected to achieve your goal of being a successful published author.

3. Believe in yourself. You *are* good enough and your book will be amazing!

Chapter Fourteen

With persistence success is inevitable!

"Six-and-a-half years of heartbreak, mourning, confusion, disappointment, discouragement, rejection, hope, clarity and a burning desire had led me to one of the greatest achievements of my life. I am so grateful I kept going when I could have easily given up — I am so proud that I kept dancing!"

It reached a point, through my decision to 'dance until it rains', that I was no longer worried about whether it would happen. The only question in my mind was when it would happen. I knew it would, I just had no idea it would take so long. But, like any journey, as long as you keep going, you will finally arrive — it's inevitable!

I can remember the day very clearly. It was one of those special days you never forget. I'd just got out of the shower and was wandering around the house in my towel — as you do. My phone started ringing. I could hear it, but I didn't know where it was. So imagine me running around the house in my towel looking for my phone! I finally found and answered it and to be honest I wasn't expecting this call.

It was a well-known Australian literary agent who had read my manuscript and actually enjoyed it! She told me she saw some potential and would help find me a publisher and then she asked if I would be interested. I told her I would think about it — NOT! I jumped on it like a heartbeat and expressed my eternal gratitude to her. After the conversation was finished, I hung up the phone and stood there stunned with a towel around my waist — it was really happening! Laura asked me if I was okay so I told her and together we jumped up and down, and danced around the room for the next five–ten minutes. At this stage, after all the jumping and without even realising it, the towel was on the floor!

Not long after that phone call, in July 2009 a publishing house accepted my manuscript —nearly five years after I decide to write this book! I was so unbelievably excited. Finally my dream was coming true. I flew to Sydney to meet with the publishers who shared my excitement and then immediately put me in contact with the managing editor to fine tune the manuscript and make a few minor adjustments — or so I thought!

The editor read the manuscript thoroughly and sent me an email. She started the email with these exact words: 'I've put some very rough ideas down for how I think the manuscript and general approach needs to be reworked', and she finished the same email with these exact words: 'Hopefully I haven't shocked you into depression!' I wasn't depressed. I was, however, overwhelmed, but I was also incredibly excited!

The way I had originally written the manuscript was separated into two sections: the first section was the story of my mother's life, while the second section was a 'how-to' on staying positive, happy and healthy. The feedback from the editor was that the second half of the book was 'same-old, same-old'. It was similar to many other books in the market place. She told me the uniqueness of the book, and the thing that would be most compelling, was my mother's story.

She suggested that I expand on my mother's story, get rid of the how-to section and then simply weave the lessons and messages throughout the story. This was very different for me as I didn't really consider myself a story-teller, which may have been some lingering doubts from my lack of academic, English and creative skills as a child. But as you have probably realised by now, I am someone who is willing to give anything a go. So, I did!

I worked hard to rewrite and improve a vast majority of the book. After much to-ing and fro-ing and some very confronting changes in thinking and approach to the manuscript it was finally finished. On October 29, 2010 I received an email from the editor which said, 'Just to let you know that your book is now at the printer'. On Monday January 10, 2011, almost six-and-half years after starting, I received my first finished hardcover copy of *Dance Until it Rains*!

This is one of the best feelings I have ever had in my life. Writing this book, in particular, was the most challenging but the most rewarding and, to be honest, the most healing thing I have done. Losing my mum was heartbreaking and for a long time I actually couldn't see the light at the end of the tunnel. The process of writing her story gave me a new perspective about her life and death. I could finally see the light and I could finally see the purpose.

Through my mum's life I could now see her purpose was to bring a flash of light and hope to this planet and to the people she impacted. Through her death I can now see her purpose, with me, is to share the lessons that can help many people live a great life and have a similar impact on many others. When I really understood this I could think about my mum, not with sadness, but with joy and gratitude. She is not gone, she is with me every day and, whilst I miss her physical presence incredibly, I believe that together we are changing the world.

Since the time of the book's release in March 2011 I know it has made a difference in many lives, none the least mine. Here are some of the comments from people who have read *Dance Until It Rains*:

In May 2010 I was diagnosed with breast cancer. I have just read your book 'Dance until it Rains'. You could have written that book about me — everything you said about your mum describes me even down to my love of pelicans. I too am seeking peace and tranquillity in my life after a lifetime of turmoil within myself. This book has had a massive impact on me and reinforces the decisions I am making and I thank you for writing it.

Many thanks for 'Dance Until It Rains'. Your mother's journey has made a profound effect on my life. I'm on my way to optimal health. Once again thank you not just for myself but all of those around me.

Thank you for the fantastic book 'Dance Until It Rains'. As you know I purchased the book yesterday morning and had finished it by tea time last night. I am not a person big on 'self help books' and have many on the shelf that I have bought but not read so it was a surprise to me that it caught my interest so easily. I imagined this would be an inspiring story of your mother's battle with cancer and that is what appealed to me. It was so much more than that. It was uplifting, inspiring, very easy to read and understand and the lessons as I think you said were all things you already knew but were written in a way that made it real. I will be reading this again and again and hope that I can apply even a few of your mother's lessons to my own life. Cheers.

—

Such a moving account of your special mother, with all those positive messages! The way you have put it together, with the well chosen quotes and your writing style (including your impish sense of humour) is such a credit to you. I think perhaps my pick of the quotes is the one at the beginning of Ch 18: "Life is not measured by the number of breaths you take, but by what takes your breath away" — Hilary Cooper. What an emotional discovery it was for me that you STARTED writing the book two months before your dear Mum passed away. So many things impressed. Overall what wonderful genes you have inherited from such great parents. Andrew, this shines through ... that a son would do this for, and about, his Mum."

Six-and-a-half years of heartbreak, mourning, confusion, disappointment, discouragement, rejection, hope, clarity and burning desire had led me to one of the greatest achievements of my life. I am so grateful that I kept going when I could have easily given up — I am so proud that I kept dancing!

Secret author's business ... the steps to success:

Can you even begin to imagine what it will feel like when your book is published and you are holding it in your hands? It was that vision along with my burning desire to get it done, no matter what, that led me to the achievement of a dream. Have you burnt that vision into your brain, your heart and your soul? Can you feel the powerful emotions associated with successfully achieving your goal?

This chapter is really to remind you, reinforce and encourage you to keep going — no matter what. You will be so incredibly glad you did. Your life will change for the better in so many ways.

Key questions and actions steps:

1. Describe what it means to you to be holding your published book in your hands.

2. What would be the consequences if you never finished this job and couldn't hold that published book in your hands?

3. Would that worry you?

4. Will you keep going, irrespective of the obstacles, the challenges and your other commitments, until it is a reality?

5. Believe me — you are good enough!

The result of dancing until it rains!

e-book

With my dad.

In store again!

Chapter Fifteen

The people you will meet and the lives you will touch

"I couldn't quite believe that Olivia Newton-John would actually take the time to call me — what a classy lady! I was on cloud nine for the rest of the weekend and again I knew deep in my heart that I could make a difference in this world!"

I want to have a global impact! I want to leave this world a better place than it was before I came into it. Am I still being crazy and illogical as I always have? I probably am, but I don't really care what other people think. In 1997 Apple came up with an advertisement that has inspired me ever since I heard it:

Here's to the crazy ones. The misfits. The rebels. The troublemakers. The round pegs in the square holes. The ones who see things differently. They're not fond of rules. And they have no respect for the status quo. You can praise them, disagree with them, quote them, disbelieve them, glorify or vilify them. About the only thing you can't do is ignore them. Because they change things. They invent. They imagine. They heal. They explore. They create. They inspire. They push the human race forward. Maybe they have to be crazy. How else can you stare at an empty canvas and see a work of art? Or sit in silence and hear a song that's never been written? Or gaze at a red planet and see a laboratory on wheels? While some see them as the crazy ones, we see genius. **Because the people who are crazy enough to think they can change the world, are the ones who do***.*

Through my writing, I believed then as I still do, that I can make a massive difference in this world. After *Dance Until It Rains* was released I decided I wanted to support a charity and donate a percentage of all book sales to that charity. After much thought, I decided to support the Olivia Newton-John Cancer and Wellness Centre in Melbourne. So, amongst other things I donated a percentage of all of my book sales to this cause. From the moment I made that decision I started to think how amazing it would be if I could get a copy of my book *Dance Until It Rains* into Olivia Newton-John's hands.

Not longer after this idea entered my brain, I received a message from a friend saying that Olivia would be at the Melbourne Cricket Ground (MCG) the next day, and there was an opportunity for a select few people to meet her before an AFL match that night. That law of attraction thing again! I thought this could be my opportunity, so I sprang into action. I made some calls and found out Olivia was performing at the MCG before the game and as a fundraising event there were 100 tickets at $500 each to get some VIP treatment, food, good seats for the game and the possibility of meeting Olivia. I didn't care about the other stuff, I paid the $500 for the Wellness Centre so I could meet Olivia and give her my book!

I already had other plans for that night but the decision

was a 'no-brainer'. I had to go and get in front of Olivia and this was an opportunity I couldn't ignore. So on the Friday night I made my way to the MCG for this event ... no no, I went to meet Olivia.

It was a pleasant enough evening, but I had only one thought on my mind. We were told that Olivia was on a tight schedule and that whilst she would come and say 'hi' to the group of 100 before she performed, it may not be possible for her to meet us all personally. Ha, that's what they think! When the time came to meet Olivia it was exciting and the adrenaline was pumping.

She arrived, she spoke briefly to the group and as soon as she had finished speaking she walked off to get ready to perform, so with one-eyed focus, I pushed my way through the crowd, got right in front of her and introduced myself. I explained, as quickly as I could, who I was, what I was aspiring to and then I handed her my two books. She was very friendly and seemed grateful for the gift. I then asked if I could get a photo taken, she said 'yes' and so I asked a man who was standing nearby if he would take a photo with my iPhone for me. He agreed for which I was grateful. I thanked Olivia and walked off feeling amazing that I had achieved what I had come to do and even had a photo to prove it!

I excitedly went to look at the photo on my phone only to discover, with absolute horror, that the man hadn't taken a photo at all! Obviously not a smart phone user! The picture wasn't there and Olivia had gone and it was too late to take another. Aaaagh! What now? Panic set in, but there had to be a solution. There always is! As I was pondering my newest dilemma, a woman I had met that night was scrolling through the photos she had taken and, just at that second I looked at her camera, guess who I saw? Correct, it was a photo of Olivia and me that she had taken! Another opportunity! I begged and she agreed to send me the photo during the next week. A few days later a very important photo appeared in my email inbox and boy, was I happy!

Stay tuned ...that's not quite the end of the story!

Soon after that evening at the MCG with Olivia and the release of *Dance Until It Rains*, in June 2011, I organised a stand at the Body, Mind and Spirit Expo in Melbourne. It was a weekend event and my goal was to sell some books.

On the Saturday morning of the expo, about 15 minutes before the doors were scheduled to open a lady came to tell me there was a gentleman out the front who would like to have a chat with me. It was not a great time, but I was intrigued, so I went out. When I got there, a man named Colin came to greet me. He shook my hand and with passion and tears in his eyes told me that he was a farmer from Western Australia who had heard me talking on the ABC radio about my book. He went out straight away and bought a copy of the book. He explained to me, with tears in his eyes, that he had lost his wife to cancer four years earlier and that my book had been so incredibly and positively impacting on him and his life.

So much so that he went out and bought copies for his family. He told me that he happened to be visiting Melbourne this particular weekend to see his children and heard that I was at the expo, so he went out of his way to come and meet me. As he was telling me all this we both stood there with tears in our eyes — an instant bond was created and a new friendship for life. It powerfully reinforced again to me why I love writing so much. I was so incredibly grateful that I could make such a difference in Colin's life — a man I never even knew or never would have known if it wasn't for my book!

The expo was fun, exciting but crazy! There were people everywhere and it was chaotic. I was on my feet for 12 hours per day for four days straight. It was amazing as I met some fabulous people and was able to take the first step in getting my message out to the world.

During that same Saturday, as I was running from 'pillar-to-post' selling books and handing out information, I noticed my phone ringing. I obviously couldn't answer it but I could see the number and that it was an international call. I was intrigued for a split second and then swamped so I didn't think it about again until I got a short lunch break several hours later.

I sat down to eat a sandwich and I inquisitively listened to the message that was left on the phone. This is what it said, word-for-word:

Hi Andrew, it's Olivia Newton-John … how are you? I just wanted to thank you for your books and the lovely thought of bringing me the books. I have started reading Dance Until It Rains and my friend is enjoying the chocolate one — ha ha ha — very much! I hope to get a chance to read them properly when I am flying home, but I just wanted to thank you for that and wish you every bit of good luck with them. I hope you will continue to be healthy and happy and thank you so much. Be well, bye-bye.

I sat there dumbfounded for several minutes. Was I dreaming? Did that really happen? I couldn't quite believe that Olivia Newton-John would actually take the time to call me — what a classy lady! I was on cloud nine for the rest of the weekend and again I knew deep in my heart that I can make a difference in this world!

Secret author's business ... the steps to success:

Your book is not the be-all-and-end-all. Your book is a tool to create positive change in your life and the lives of others. I see far too often champions, like you, go through all the sacrifice, persistence and challenges to write and publish their book ... then it sits in a box with hundreds or thousand of others, in the garage for the next however many years.

Your book is a tool to help people through certain aspects of their life — use it! A hammer is a tool, but it is of no value if it isn't used to plant a nail, connecting two surfaces to create something of value. Your book needs to be in someone's hands so it can get into their head and heart and have the impact you wish it to have. Now is the time to start thinking big because you will have a global impact if you choose to. I say it again and I need you to hear and believe it — you are good enough to change the world!

Key questions and actions steps:

1. What good would you like to do in this world if you believed you could do anything?

2. How would you make the world a better place?

3. What message do you want to share with the world?

4. What causes would you like to support with your book?

5. What are some ways you could start to spread the word about your book?

6. Do you have a website, social media presence and can you spread the word digitally?

7. What groups are you affiliated with who can help you spread the word through their existing networks?

8. Find someone to help you in this process if you need to.

Olivia speaking — I'm just waiting for my chance!

'The photo'

Laura with the book at the Olivia Newton-John Cancer & Wellness Centre in Melbourne.

At the Mind Body Spirit Expo, June 2011.

With Colin, my new friend from WA.

Chapter Sixteen

Getting off my butt to spread the word!

"I stepped down from the pedestal I had placed myself upon, slapped myself a few times, shook off the ego I had not yet deserved to be carrying and decided to get into action."

So, here I was, at that time, a very passionate and excited published author. I had three published books to my name, some very positive signs and make no mistake about it, I had visions of fame, fortune and grandeur! I had publishers who had developed a PR and marketing campaign. I had set up a website with my books available for purchase and I had sent out an email to my massive database (well, my modest database!). Then I sat there with my feet up on my desk, rubbing my hands together waiting for the flood of speaking opportunities, book orders and royalty payments to come flowing in but ... they didn't come!

What's wrong? Where's the action? Where are the sales? Where's the fame and fortune? I rang the publishers and demanded to know why they weren't selling more books and bringing in more opportunities for me. Sure they had got some print media exposure and radio interviews but I wanted to know why it wasn't translating into sales?

They let me rant and rave, they waited patiently until I finished and then asked me a simple question, 'What are *you* doing to promote yourself and your book?' I responded with confidence, clarity and certainty; 'Umm, well, actually, I ... aaah, let's see, mmm ... actually ...um not much ... well, to be honest ... aaah, um .... nothing!' They listened to my empowering and uplifting speech and then politely suggested that maybe I should get 'off my excuse', get out there, start promoting the books I had written and doing something *myself* to actually create the success I wanted.

With that, I stepped down from the pedestal I had placed myself upon, slapped myself a few times, shook off the ego I had not yet deserved to be carrying and decided to get into action and support the great work the publishers were doing to promote and sell my books. Okay, so how do I do that?

I sat there for a while and thought about what I was trying to achieve and I wrote out some goals for myself. I thought about how many books I wanted to sell and I developed a list of ideas that could help make this happen. I then put together a basic action plan and as horrible and uncomfortable as it was, I got into action!

It's an amazing principle of life that when you get into action, all of a sudden, positive things start to happen — almost like magic. As I started to reach out to people to discuss ways I could add value to them through my speaking and my books, people started to contact me! How does that work? I didn't know, but I was happy for it nevertheless.

The best example of this happened in the very early

stages of this frightening process. I decided I would try to get as many speaking gigs as I could — it seemed a logical first step. I returned to the speaking agencies that had told me to come back when I had published books. So, with three published books, I proudly went back to them and presented myself as a fabulously successful author and speaker. They put me on their books, on their website and told me they would do the best they could but also said not to hold my breath nor rely solely on them. That was good advice as I had sat around twiddling my thumbs and waiting for things to just appear for too long already.

I sat down in front of my computer and went to the place where all people eventually go ... Google yet again. I thought, as a starting point, I would approach business groups who put on speakers at their regular business networking breakfasts and meetings. I found an online directory with hundreds of these groups, I put my fear in my pocket and started calling.

You can imagine the response I heard 95 per cent of the time — 'No', 'Not today', 'No thanks', 'Send me your info and we will get back to you' blah, blah, blah! It was lucky I had been here before and I understood the process. I knew it was a numbers game, so I kept going. Hearing 'no' is never fun and it can get quite discouraging, but I knew what I had to offer was amazing and I had faith it would lead to a positive result.

I reached one particular business networking group on the list and with sweat dripping and my heart racing I dialled the number. It was answered by a gentleman who did not give me the warm and friendly reception I was hoping for, but I surged ahead anyway. 'Hi, my name is Andrew Jobling. I am an author and speaker and was wondering if you are ever looking for speakers for the events you run?' Not surprisingly, his response was not positive. In fact it was quite hostile. He told me in no uncertain terms he wasn't interested and that they sourced their speakers from within their own network. He hung up! Okay then ... that would be another, 'No'!

A bit shook up from that call, I decided to go and have a drink of water and get some fresh air before I came back for another self-inflicted session of rejection and abuse! Ten minutes later my phone rang. It was that same angry gentleman who had just given me my worst rejection so far. He was different. He was friendly and apologetic for his behaviour. He told me that as soon as he'd hung up, he'd Googled my name and saw that I had played for the St. Kilda Football Club — the club he supported.

We chatted for a while mostly about football! I found out about his group and I explained my situation. I proposed to him what I had to offer and he told me he would love to have me come and speak. One month later I was standing on the stage at the Crown Casino Palladium Ballroom in Melbourne speaking to 250 people. At that event I met several people that have led me to more speaking opportunities, book sales and other wonderful events.

This initial event was in November 2008 and since that time I have worked closely with that wonderful gentleman and we have become great friends. I have been closely involved with the business groups he has developed all around the country. It has been and still is an incredibly mutually beneficial business relationship that will last for many decades to come. All this started from one of the most terrifying and seemingly negative phone conversations I have ever had.

From that early uncomfortable point I have gradually grown in confidence, skills and expectancy. Even today, I still don't enjoy cold-calling and it still terrifies me, but I know the results I get from it, so ... I keep doing it. Since then I have been able to effectively get speaking gigs within existing organisations, run many public workshops and seminars, created some amazing strategic alliances, contributed to many websites, magazines and newspapers, run my own radio show, got my head around social media and many other strategies that have lifted my profile and helped me sell more books.

One of the best decisions I made was to start writing a weekly article, now blog and send it out to my database. Over the years, to this current time (November 2014), I have written and sent out over 450 articles/blogs. Initially, I wasn't sure whether it was worth the valuable time I was spending on it. I was getting advised by many people there were more important things I could be doing with my time. However, I stuck at it and it has proven to be one of the most valuable activities I have done and will continue to do, and for reasons that are not immediately obvious.

Firstly, it added value to my database. Secondly, it developed a great discipline and habit of weekly writing. Thirdly, it helped me develop content for other books, e-books and newspaper/magazine articles. Fourthly, it has helped me build my database numbers and a relationship of trust with my database. Finally, the serendipities that have resulted over the years include; sales of many books, speaker bookings on numerous occasions, many mentoring clients and, most importantly, the joy of knowing that I am making a difference in the lives of others. These all came from subscribers and regular readers of my blogs who, resonated with a particular blog when the timing was right, then contacted me for my help and support.

Again I am grateful for the struggle and discomfort I forced myself through as it has led me to some amazing experiences and achievements that I wouldn't trade for anything.

Secret author's business ... the steps to success:

Whether you have self-published or traditionally published your book you need to take responsibility and action to get it sold and successful. If you have self-published you are on your own and need to really take notice of the next steps I will outline. If you have traditionally published you will partner with the publishers and work with them to really accelerate profile and sales.

Selling is rarely comfortable but is a necessity. So, please take this from the supportive and positive place it is coming from — get over it and get on with it! The people who dislike selling don't really believe that the product or service they represent will enhance the purchaser's life in some way. The sooner you passionately believe that you, your book and your message will positively impact the lives of all people, the sooner promoting and selling will become simple and fun.

Key questions and actions steps:

1. Do you really believe your book will make a positive difference in the lives of others? Why?

2. Are you ready to set some goals around promoting and selling your book?
   a. How many books do you have?
   b. How many do you want to sell?
   c. In what time frame?
   d. Why do you want to sell them?
   e. How will you feel when they are sold?
   f. In what way will selling them impact your life?
   g. What will you do next?

3. What are you prepared to do to make the sales?

4. Use some or all of the following strategies. Get help if you need to:
   a. Write a press/media release.
   b. Develop a dynamic, interactive and compelling website.
   c. Hold a book launch.
   d. Use social media.
   e. Organise editorials and articles in local papers.
   f. Write regular blogs or articles and build a database.
   g. Get celebrity endorsement.
   h. Get book reviews, write articles for magazines, newspapers and websites.
   i. Get on TV and radio.
   j. Do talks for groups, schools and/or organisations.

5. If you are self-publishing you will also need to explore distribution, getting into stores and e-book format options.

6. Have fun. This is character building and some of the best relationships of your life will come out of this.

Chapter Seventeen

If I can do it ... anyone can!

"I just thought about the one quality I have ... I will always finish what I start! That is my secret! It is the answer to any question, any dilemma and the achievement of any desire. I knew beyond any shadow of doubt that if I just kept going, kept learning, kept getting up and staying focussed on the end result success would not be accidental, it would be inevitable."

I had written and published three books that were all selling and making a difference. Who would have ever possibly imagined it? Certainly not I or most of the people who knew me! I mean here was little ol' me with no writing skills, no experience, no real specific education to speak of, no time and no idea about what I was doing yet I became a successful published author. It was, and still is, quite mind-blowing!

I just thought about the one quality I have; I will always finish what I start! That is my secret! It is the answer to any question, any dilemma and the achievement of any desire. I knew beyond any shadow of doubt that if I just kept going, kept learning, kept getting up and staying focussed on the end result ... success would not be accidental, it would be inevitable.

I then received this email:

*I finished reading 'Dance Until It Rains', I absolutely loved it ... I couldn't put it down. I am so glad you got it finished! Your mum was a wonderfully inspirational woman. Your book has made me even **more determined to tell my story**.*

This person was determined to tell her story. Hmmm, how many other people would love to either tell their story or write a book of some sort? I was sure there were lots of them. At that time, however, I had no idea just how many! I started asking people and the majority of them indicated an interest in telling their story, or the story of someone close to them. An idea came into my head.

I knew, through the process of writing about my mum and feedback from many people, that everybody has a story that needs to be shared and will inspire others. I then realised the obvious — if I can be an author then anybody can be an author and I mean *anybody* and *everybody*!

I decided I was going share this accidental, new found passion with others to encourage and help them to experience the same joy I now experience. So I developed a workshop called *One Word at a Time* specifically designed to help anyone, no matter their background, age, education, skill level or self-belief to write and publish and sell their own book. My reasoning was simple — if I can do it, anyone can do it. Everyone has a book in them that needs to be written and shared.

The reality is that all it takes to write a book is just one word at a time! The key factor for me has never been ability, technique, literary knowledge or most other things that people believe it takes to be an author, as I never had any of those attributes. For me it was simple; start writing, one word at a time, and keep going until it is finished — that is it. The simple secret of success is to finish what you start!

I found a venue, set a date, created a promotional flyer, sent out emails to my contact list, got on the phone and heavily promoted this workshop. I had a vision of hundreds of people filling the room — so many, in fact, that I would need to put on another date or find a bigger venue! After several weeks of serious PR and all out effort I had six people booked for the workshop. Okay, maybe not as grand as I had imagined ... but a start nevertheless.

It was fun, I shared with those six people exactly what I had done to write and publish my books. I was passionate about my message and they seemed to get a lot of out it and really enjoy the workshop. I was having a great time being the centre of attention ... again! Then an amazing thing happened. Two of those six people actually did what I suggested. It was amazing; I was in a classroom where people actually listened to me! Soon after those two people, Natalie and Alan, had a published book.

I had totally surprised myself again. Not only can I write a book, but I can help others do the same and so a new passion had began. This is what my first two published authors said about the workshop:

Andrew's course showed me how the whole book writing process works. In practical terms I was shown what makes for a good book, how it keeps readers engaged and what is most likely to be appealing in today's many readership markets. The course also helped me to set a personal plan, which when I strayed from it, brought me back on track. It addressed not just the mechanics of good writing but helped me to identify why I wanted to write and what my book meant to me personally. — Alan

When I started on the journey to write my book I met Andrew Jobling and attended one of his workshops. There were two things he said that made the difference for me to get my book written and published. The first was to 'start with the end in mind' and the second was to 'finish what I start' ... that's exactly what I did. I would recommend his workshop to anyone wanting to be a published author. — Natalie

I was hooked! I set up several more face-to-face workshops and worked really hard to get just a handful of people at each one. I still loved it, as did the attendees, and more published authors have resulted. I wanted to impact more people, but started to realise the limitations of face-to-face workshops: they were costly, took a lot of time and effort to promote and were limited to people available at specific dates and times in a very restricted location.

I thought about travelling to do more of these workshops but if I could only get six people at a workshop in my own home town, how would I go anywhere else? There was only one solution, and one I didn't have much knowledge about or practical experience with — the internet!

Secret author's business ... the steps to success:

What I have learned and what I teach is that writing a book, apart from being an amazingly wonderful thing to do, will be a catalyst for potentially significant and positive changes in your career and life. There is no way, when I published my first book, I could have foreseen the direction my life was going to take, the fabulous things that I would be doing and the incredible things I would have been able to achieve.

For me the passion became helping other people write books — for you it will be something completely different. Just know that writing your book will expand your thinking, strengthen your self-belief, give you a vision, open doors that you may never have considered and literally explode your career and your life. It will do this, as I love to say ... one word at a time!

Imagine if you could change your current circumstances. Imagine getting yourself out of the nine-five, eight-six or whatever your current rat-race is. Imagine if you could transform your career and do something that aligns totally with your values, feeds your passion and fulfills your purpose in life. It happened to me and I truly believe it can be the same for you. Your book will be the catalyst for incredible positive change — trust me.

Key questions and actions steps:

1. If you could choose your career and how you earned your income what would it look like?

2. Do you believe your book can help to bring this to a wonderful reality?

3. What skills, strengths and abilities will writing a book help you to develop?

4. What direction can you see your book helping you to take?

5. Who can you ask to help develop a career path strategy and keep you on track and accountable to make it happen?

6. Are you willing to commit to this strategy?

My first author: Lindsay Tighe.

My second author:
Natalie Ashdown.

My third author:
Alan Roe.

Chapter Eighteen

'One Word at a Time' goes global!

"I learned a new and very exciting word — 'leverage'!
We started to take the workshop to existing global online
platforms and offered them a commission to sell it.
We leveraged other websites, we leveraged their traffic and the
workshop sales exploded beyond any and all of my wildest dreams."

An online workshop ... hmmm, could I? I knew very little about the internet with the exception of the basics: opening a web browser, using Google and sending an email! How could I possibly create an online program? Then I thought back to my decision to write a book. I was in pretty much in the same situation. I had no idea, but I did it anyway! That being the case, I decided I could do it. How, I wasn't sure but I didn't want to be bogged down with details!

The only way I could ever take this workshop to the world was online so the 'how' was actually irrelevant. I always remember back to my professional football days — if you want something bad enough and you are prepared to work, learn and 'keep dancing' then a successful outcome is inevitable. With this in mind, and a burning desire to get it done, I mapped out a plan and started writing ten online modules.

I had written the welcome module and the first two modules of ten when the Body Mind and Spirit Expo in Melbourne, I had booked a stand at, came around. It was Laura's idea that, in addition to promoting *Dance Until It Rains*, we start promoting the online workshop ... even though I still had eight more modules to write! I have learned through the years that agreeing with my wife is a smart idea! So, whilst tentative about this, seemingly premature launch of a program that hadn't been written and, in the name of marital harmony, I did it anyway.

We designed a pull-up banner with the question, 'Everyone has a book in them ... what's yours?' We printed surveys and asked people to fill them in. Amazingly, over the four days almost 400 surveys were completed. What blew me away was that, out of all the surveys completed, more than 300 of them indicated they wanted to write a book. As always my wife knows best!

But then panic set in.

Why? I had to write an online workshop and I had to do it fast. I quickly put up a landing and booking page on my website www.andrewjobling.com.au/one-word-at-a-time/ to cater for any of these people who were motivated to get started — there were and they did! Then I started writing fast! Talk about a steep learning curve. All within a few days after that expo I learned how do the back-end management of my website, create content, upload instead of download, create YouTube videos and embed them into the site, create flipbooks, embed booking forms and much, much more. My head was spinning, my fingers were numb and I was sleep deprived but I had to keep going because people, who had started the program, were catching up to me!

At one stage a lady actually caught up to me and requested a module I hadn't finished writing yet! A little baby white lie about technical difficulties and in a couple of days I was back in control of the situation. Finally the program was written and the online course was officially launched.

After that initial surge from the Body Mind and Spirit Expo I was excited and knew that big things were about to happen so again, I sat back and expected sales and bookings to just roll in. You would think I would have already learned this lesson! I leaned back on my chair, put my feet up on the desk, felt very proud of myself and waited, and waited, and waited ...and waited! Where were all the bookings? Where were all these people who wanted to write a book? What had I done wrong?

I actually hadn't done anything wrong, I just had to learn another lesson. The lesson: a landing page on a website is one thing, but getting traffic to that website is something else totally!

So, how do I get people to my site? At that point, again with the help of my wonderful wife, I learned a new and very exciting word — 'leverage'! We started to take the workshop to existing global online platforms and offered them a commission to sell it. We leveraged other websites, we leveraged their traffic and the workshop sales exploded beyond any and all of my wildest dreams.

In the first three weeks of this new strategy I had sold over 1000 workshops around Australia! Since that time (late 2011) and until now (November 2014) well over 7000 people all around the world are at some stage of the 10-module workshop and I am proud to say that, so far, at least 35 people (that I know of) as a result of my workshop have written and published their very own book. These are people, who like me, had no idea they could! They didn't know how to, they just knew why they wanted to. As a result they are now changing lives of people they don't even know! Can you see why this is such an incredible passion for me?

My rapidly growing database, positive results and fabulous feedback meant I had more traffic to my website and could now promote and run face-to-face workshops that would actually attract bums on seats! I was even more attractive as a speaker because learning how to write a book is something people want to here about.

I was invited to speak at an event in early 2014. At that event and after I had finished speaking I met a couple who have helped me take this whole amazing journey to another exciting level, which I'll tell you more about in the next chapter.

Secret author's business ... the steps to success:

None of us think as big as we could and should. What is it about life that puts a lid on our thinking and a limit to what we believe we are capable of achieving? If you are reading this section, at this stage of this book then I want to encourage you to take off the lid and let your imagination start flowing wildly.

Ignore the advice of small-minded people who are living an average life. Erase the memory of a school teacher, relative or friend who told you to be realistic. Dismiss any thoughts that taking risks is a bad thing. Remove the idea from your brain that you need to avoid failure. I want to encourage you to go for it ... whatever it may be for you.

Do you want to have an internationally acclaimed best-selling book? You can. Do you want to sell your book in multiple languages and have it impact millions of lives? You will. Do you want to stand on a stage and speak in front of tens of thousands of people? You can make it happen. Do you want a website or online program that goes viral and creates enormous wealth? You are good enough to do it.

Are you with me? Remember what Steve jobs said, "...the people who are crazy enough to think they can change the world, are the ones who do."

Key questions and actions steps:

1. If you really believed you could do anything what would it be?

2. When you let your imagination run wild, what can you see?

3. How do you feel when you imagine it?

4. Start writing a description of this audacious dream, read it every day and start to think about what you would need to do to bring it into reality.

5. Do something every day to make it happen!

One Word at a Time Online workshop.

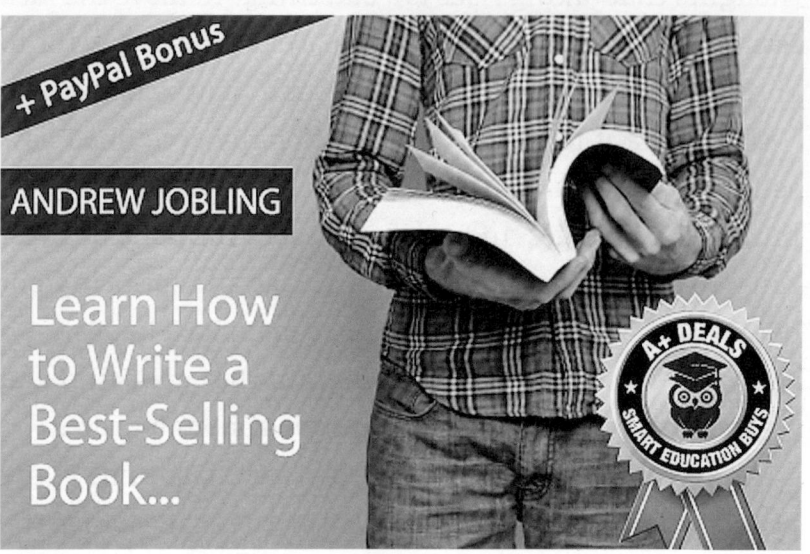
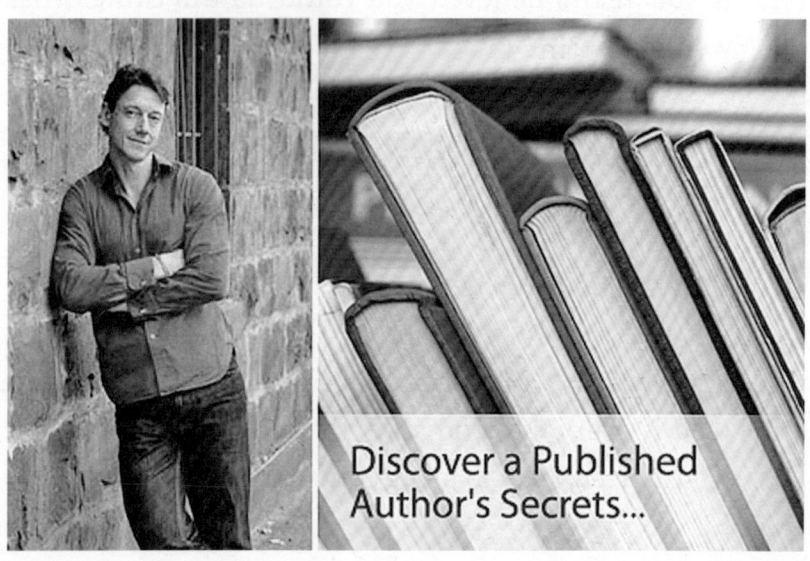

Chapter Nineteen

The universe always delivers

"There is a universal principle called the 'law of attraction' and, I don't know about you, but I deeply believe it is a very positive and powerful law ... if we choose to harness it in the right way. It basically states that you will attract into your life what you give you attention to and focus on."

The online workshop had performed incredibly well, but things were starting to slow down a little. I was living in the former glory and success of the workshop and hadn't thought much more beyond that. Like everything in life we need to keep evolving, improving, and enhancing what we are doing or we will become extinct. I wasn't worried about becoming extinct, but I did know that something needed to change but what it was, I wasn't sure.

There is a universal principle called the 'law of attraction' and, I don't know about you, but I deeply believe it is a very positive and powerful law ... if we choose to harness it in the right way. It basically states that you will attract into your life what you give you attention to and focus on.

If you focus on things you don't want, you will attract what you don't want! Have you ever got up in the morning, stubbed your toe, bumped your head and said, 'This is going to a bad day'? Then one bad thing after another happened and you thought is was luck — wrong! You expected bad things to happen and they did. It was the law of attraction! Have you ever had days when everything goes amazingly well and you couldn't understand why? That wasn't luck either — you were thinking positive thoughts and attracted them into your life.

So early in 2014 I was thinking about and focused on how I take this workshop, helping more people write and publish books, to the next level. I knew I could help people write the book, but the major challenge many of these people were facing was getting their work published. It really seemed to be a tough stage, as I have already discussed, and many were getting disillusioned and lost in this process. I was wondering how I could solve this challenge — what would Vinnie do?

Soon after this initial thought I was invited to speak at an event and when I had finished I was, amazingly and coincidentally, approached by a man who owned a publishing company. I met him and his partner, we had a brief chat, I took his business card and left without thinking too much more about it — why the penny didn't drop immediately I can't tell you. My mind works in mysterious ways!

The next day it hit me ... this could be perfect! They publish books. I wanted to write more books. I wanted to help people write and publish books and I was looking for a way to move to the next level — this really could be it. I was excited because I could see a way to solve my dilemma and re-launch the workshop as a more comprehensive package. I wasted no more time, got on the phone and made an appointment to meet them that week.

We sat, we talked and I couldn't quite believe how perfectly well aligned this seemed. This couple not only own and operate a successful traditional publishing house, Jojo Publishing, but a publishing house with a difference. They want to help authors get published and they want to publish books that make a difference! As they were telling me about what they were doing and their vision for the future I was getting more and more excited. Then as I explained what I was doing and my vision for the future I could see them getting excited — it just clicked. We knew from that first meeting that the universe had drawn us together and this partnership was meant to happen!

I told them I had an idea for a series of books starting with one called *Accidental Author*. (They obviously liked it!) I told them about my workshop and we saw a perfect fit. I would help people write the book and then they would help, guide and support them the whole way through the publishing, marketing and distribution process. I wish I had found these guys when I was trying to get *Dance Until It Rains* published!

As I write this we are still in only very early days but it is looking more and more promising every day. We have already run several information sessions for budding authors. We already have many people on the journey and excited about the fact that they actually can and will become successful published authors! We have plans to expand globally, we are all thinking big and we know that we can do it — thanks to the universe and our vision!

We would love for you to become part of this vision — all you have to do is simply write your book! It will be amazing and *you can do* it. How do I know? If I can do it, you most certainly can too! We then let the publishers do what they do best.

Secret author's business ... the steps to success:

If you ever saw a turtle on a fence post, you would probably ask the same questions as I would, how did it get there? It clearly didn't climb up there on its own. It must have been placed there by someone. Okay, random thought ... or is it?

I often think back about each and every step of the process to get to this point in my life. Right now, as I am finishing off my fourth published book and am helping thousands of people worldwide to write their own book, I can state categorically that I could never have done it on my own. You can do it. You will do it, but be open to the universe and find great mentors, teachers and cheerleaders to help you along the way.

There is a Buddhist proverb that states, 'when the student is ready the teacher will appear'. This is very true! When you are ready to learn, when you are ready to change and when you put it out there the universe will deliver to you the person who can help you make it happen. I am sure you have already experienced this in your life.

Put it out there, open yourself to possibility and the right people will come into your life and help you write and publish your book. Maybe someone handed you this book just as you were wondering how you could ever write your own book? The universe delivers — every single time.

Key questions and actions steps:

1. What do you need help with right now?

2. Who is currently in your life that could help you? It might be someone you have not even thought about until now?

3. Get excited about what you can achieve with the help of the right people.

4. Today — not tomorrow — call, email or message someone who has done what you want to do and ask for help.

5. Be open to the possibility that someone may appear in your life — someone who is just the person you need to help you move through a sticking point.

6. Focus on, think about and work towards what you want and the universe will be there to help you turn it into a reality

Chapter Twenty

The final word ...

"The moral to my story is that there really are no accidents in life! We create our destiny by dreaming bigger than most people would think reasonable, by believing in ourselves more than most people would think sensible, by making decisions that most people would think illogical and continuing to act way beyond the point that most people would have given up."

Great things will always come from seemingly random accidents — you just need believe it and be open to the amazing opportunities that are waiting for you. Enjoy this story:

A great king, living in medieval times, had a very loyal servant. The servant was by the king's side at all times and would pander to the king's every demand. The servant had just one slightly annoying habit, and that was every time something happened he would say, 'This is good,' no matter what the situation. This did bother the king at times, but because his servant was so attentive and loyal he would often just let it go.

One day the king decided to take his servant and go hunting and so the servant packed his sire's gun and off they went. What neither had realised is that the servant had incorrectly packed the *gun and so when the king went to shoot it ... he blew off his thumb! The servant's response to this painful and horrible event was to say, 'Ahhh, this is good'. The king, who had just lost his thumb and was suffering unbearable pain, could see no good at all. He was so angered by his servant's comment that he took him back to the castle and had him locked away and shackled in the deepest darkest dungeon in the castle.*

Twelve months later, with the servant still locked in the dungeon, the king went out hunting again. This time he was on his own and, this time, he was sure that the gun was packed correctly. Before he got a chance to use it the king was captured by natives and put in a huge cauldron of water over a raging fire as a sacrifice to the gods. But when the natives noticed that he was missing a thumb they released him as he was imperfect and not a worthy sacrifice!

The king immediately returned to the castle and had the servant released from the dungeon. He apologised to the servant saying, 'You were right losing my thumb was a good thing and what I did to you was a bad thing'. The servant responded, 'No, no that was a good thing. If I wasn't shackled in the dungeon I would have been with you ... and I have all my fingers and thumbs!'

I still laugh today when I think of what has had to happen in my life to go from where I was to a passionate writer and author. The series of events that have, seemingly by accident, led me to this point where I can now influence and help many thousands of people to do something they had no idea they wanted to do or even could do is surreal. Life is an amazing and exciting place of possibility and surprise!

The moral to my story is that there really are *no accidents* in life! We create our destiny by dreaming bigger than most people would think reasonable, by believing in ourselves more than most people would think sensible, by making decisions most people would think illogical and continuing to act way beyond the point where most people would have given up.

It is your life. Live it by choice, be open to opportunities and enjoy the seemingly accidental pleasures that come to you in abundance.

Above everything else write that book you want to write. It will be so worth it and it will change your life for the better — forever. Just know that if I can do it, trust me, you can most definitely do it too!

Secret author's business ... the steps to success:

- Are you ready to write?

- Have you been telling yourself you could and should write a book?

- Have you been putting it off?

- Are you ready to do it ... now?

- Okay then, nothing can stop you. If you act on and follow the steps outlined in this book, I promise that you will be a published author. You can do it ... I believe in you.

- If you feel you need extra support, I would love to offer you a choice of four special VIP packages and memberships to help you negotiate the challenges, enjoy the journey and get the job done.

Key questions and actions steps:

1. Get started now, don't wait any longer — simply follow through the steps outlined in this book.

2. If you need additional support, go to www.andrewjobling.com.au/one-word-at-a-time/packages/

3. If you need me, I will be in contact with you.

4. Get started.

5. Keep going until you are a published author.

You can do it!